RE

Sou

Spanish Proverbs

REFRANES
Southwestern
Spanish Proverbs

COLLECTED
AND TRANSLATED
BY

Rubén Cobos

MUSEUM OF NEW MEXICO PRESS
SANTA FE

To my children, Evelia, Irving,
Hélène, Renée, and Rubén.

Printed in the United States of America.

10 9 8 7 6 5

Library of Congress Cataloging in Publication Data
Main entry under title:

Refranes: Southwestern Spanish proverbs.

Rev. ed. of: Southwestern Spanish proverbs.
Bibliography: p.
Includes indexes.
1. Proverbs, Spanish—Southwest, New. I. Cobos,
Rubén. II. Southwestern Spanish proverbs.
PN6495.U5R4   1985   398'.9'61   84-18998
ISBN 0-89013-177-5

Design and illustrations by Daniel Martinez.

Museum of New Mexico Press
P.O. Box 2087
Santa Fe, New Mexico 87503

Contents

Preface

Some of the proverbs included in this work come from towns and villages in northern New Mexico and southern Colorado. They were gathered while I was teaching at the University of New Mexico in Albuquerque and are a part of my collection of Southwest Indo-Hispanic folklore. Other proverbs were contributed by my students from Texas (San Antonio and El Paso), Arizona (Globe), and California (San José and Mountainview).

The word *refranes* (proverbs) is used in the title of the book because it is the accepted literary term for this type of folk expression throughout the Spanish-speaking world. Spelling and accentuation of all entries in Spanish conform with the latest norms for standard Spanish orthography. Archaisms and other regionally developed vocabulary (*alesnas, jierve, mojo, troja, truje,* etc.), appear in italics throughout the text.

The refranes are listed in alphabetical sequence with a literal translation given for each entry. This is then followed by the corresponding proverb in English or by an explanation of the meaning of the Spanish folk saying: A donde fueres, haz lo que vieres. (Wherever you go, do as you see.) When in Rome, do as the Romans do.

An index of subjects in Spanish and English is provided at the end of the book. This part of the work is intended to save time in locating a proverb when the reader may only remember or be aware of the general subject.

I wish to thank all informants, and particularly my students in Southwest folklore classes, for their invaluable help in realizing this modest contribution to the field of Southwest Indo-Hispanic folklore. I would also like to express my deepest appreciation to the staff at the Museum of New Mexico Press, James Mafchir, publisher, and Sarah Nestor and Martha Baca, editors, for their expertise and valuable help.

Introduction

A proverb can be defined as a self-contained speech unit that expresses a truth or some bit of folk wisdom in language that is simple and invariably picturesque. Proverbs have an air of spontaneity and overtness, and their meaning or intention is readily grasped by the listener. They are further characterized by brevity of form and frugality of words used in conveying their message: Silence is golden. All that glitters is not gold. When the cat's away, the mice will play. A bird in the hand is worth two in the bush.

In English proverbs are often referred to as *sayings*, as can be seen in the expression "as the saying goes" after a proverb has been stated: Out of sight, out of mind (as the saying goes). In Spanish one finds an analogous situation. The Spanish name for proverb is *refrán*, which is also alluded to as a *dicho* (saying). The word dicho, like the English term saying, is also often used after a refrán: Ama a tu prójimo como a ti mismo (como dice el dicho). (Love thy neighbor as thyself [as the saying goes]). Proverbs and sayings in English, and refranes and dichos in Spanish, then, are synonymous and interchangeable terms; however, the folk seem to prefer to use the word *saying* rather than *proverb* in English, and *dicho* rather than *refrán* in Spanish.

In addition to these terms, and unknown to themselves, people include among their sayings many witicisms and proverbial expressions written by the great writers and thinkers of the past, such as Hippocrates, Pythagoras, Agricola, and Erasmus. These include adages, apothegms, aphorisms (rules for living a healthy life), axioms, maxims, and sentences such as the following:[1] An idle man is the devil's ear. If you wish to live a long life, check your appetite. Caesar's wife is above suspicion.

The proverbs of Solomon, found in *Proverbs* and *Ecclesiastes*, fall in this category. These were commanded to be collected by King Solomon, who gave them a literary status and had them put in writing for posterity. The following Solomonic proverbs now form part of oral tradition: Like father, like son. Spare the rod and spoil the child. Necessity knows no law. An eye for an eye and a tooth for a tooth. Wisdom is more precious than rubies. Wealth makes friends.

People turn to their proverbs in times of need and tribulation: En tus apuros y afanes, acude a tus refranes. (In time of need, turn to your proverbs.) They use them also as guidelines for the development of attitudes, moral values, and social behavior. They look to them for advice and for examples of such qualities as discretion, charity, and patience:

Advice:	Buen abogado, mal vecino.
	(Good lawyers make bad neighbors.)
	Del viejo el consejo.
	(Experience gives advice.)
	Antes que te cases, mira lo que haces.
	(Look before you leap.)
Industry:	A quien madruga, Dios le ayuda.
	(God helps an early riser.)
	Si quieres fortuna y fama, levántate de mañana.
	(The early bird catches the worm.)
Charity:	Candil de la calle y oscuridad de su casa.
	(Charity begins at home.)
	Haz bien y no acates a quién.
	(Charity is its own reward.)
Discretion:	Hay veces que vale más ser gallina que gallo.
	(Discretion is the better part of valor.)
Social behavior:	Vale más solo que mal acompañado.
	(Better alone than in bad company.)
	Dime con quién andas y te diré quién eres.
	(A man is known by the company he keeps.)
Patience:	Con paciencia se comió el piojo a la pulga.
	(It takes patience to achieve one's ends.)
	Un solo golpe no tumba un roble.
	(Rome wasn't built in a day.)
Moral values:	Arbol que crece torcido, nunca su rama endereza.
	(As the twig is bent, so will the tree grow.)

Proverbs represent most aspects of life. They compare people to animals such as cats, dogs, horses, pigs, chickens, roosters, hawks, and pigeons and transfer the characteristics of these animals to human beings. The Spanish people, particularly, love these piquant expressions because they mirror situations in which they are direct participants. And such is their affection for their dichos that they rhyme them as they rhyme their *adivinanzas* (riddles) and include them in their stock of folk poetry: El que deja para otro día de Dios desconfía. A Dios rogando y con el mazo dando. Agarra fama y échate en la cama. Ahora es el reír, después será el reír. Amor de lejos es pa los pendejos. A careful reader will readily notice rhymes in almost fifty percent of the proverbs included in the present collection.

It is my belief that proverbs reveal the attitudes, feelings, and psychology of a people.

Rubén Cobos, professor emeritus
The University of New Mexico
October, 1984

1. An *adage* is a form in which action is emphasized or to be effected. An *apothegm* is a terse and sententious aphorism expressing the wisdom of the sages. An *aphorism* is a short and pithy sentence expressing some observation or a general truth or sentiment. An *axiom*, likewise, emphasizes a self-evident or generally accepted truth taken for granted as the basis of reasoning. A *maxim*, from *maxima sententia*, is a rule or precept sanctioned by experience and relating especially to the practical concerns of everyday life. A *sentence* is a maxim considered from a literary or oratorical point of view. (See Selected Readings.)

REFRANES
Southwestern
Spanish Proverbs

Abril lluvioso hace a mayo hermoso.
April showers bring May flowers.

1. **ABRIL lluvioso hace a mayo hermoso.** (Rainy April makes May beautiful.) *April showers bring May flowers.*

2. **A BUENA HAMBRE no hay pan duro.** (No bread is hard when one is really hungry.) *Hunger is the best sauce.*

3. **A BUEY viejo, cencerro nuevo.** (For an old ox, a new cowbell.) *Censures old men who fall in love with young women.*

4. **A BUEY viejo no le falta garrapata.** (Every old ox has his cattle tick.) *Old age is a series of ills.*

5. **A BURRO dado no se le ve el colmillo.** (Don't look at a gift burro's eye tooth.) *Don't look a gift horse in the mouth.*

6. **A CABALLO regalado no se le mira el diente.** (Don't look at a gift horse's tooth.) *Don't look a gift horse in the mouth.*

7. **ACABANDOSE EL DINERO se termina la amistad.** (When the money runs out, the friendship ends.) *While the pot boils, friendship blooms.*

8. **A CADA CAPILLITA se le llega su fiestecita.** (Every little chapel has its feast day.) *Every dog has his day.*

9. **A CADA GUAJOLOTE se le llega su Noche Buena.** (Every turkey has his Christmas Eve.) *Every dog has his day.*

10. **A CADA GUAJOLOTITO se le llega su Noche Buena.** (Every little turkey has his Christmas Eve.) *Every dog has his day.*

11. **A CADA PAJARO le gusta su nido.** (Each bird likes his nest.) *People like best what is theirs.*

12. **A CADA SANTO se le llega su función.** (Every saint has his feast day.) *Every dog has his day.*

13. **A CADA TIERRA, su uso.** (To each land, its customs.) *When you're in Rome, do as the Romans do.*

14. **A CADA UNO su gusto lo engorde.** (Let everyone get fat on his own taste.) *Everyone to his taste.*

15. **A CAMINO largo, paso corto.** (For a long journey, a short step.) *Advises one to pace oneself.*

16. **ACHAQUES quiere la muerte (para llavarse el difunto).** (Death needs no excuses to take the corpse.) *Ironically chides those who are always looking for excuses.*

17. **A CHILLIDOS de puerco, oídos de matancero.** (For a pig's squeal, a butcher's ear.) *A foolish question deserves no answer.*

18. **A COMER y a misa rezada, a la primera llamada.** (To eat and to assist Mass, at the first call.) *First things first.*

19. **A DIOS rogando y con el mazo dando.** (Praying to God but hammering.) *Trust others but depend on yourself.*

20. **ADONDE FUERES, haz lo que vieres.** (Wherever you go, do as you see.) *When in Rome, do as the Romans.*

21. **¡ADONDE IRA EL BUEY que no are!** (Where can the ox go that he is not made to plow!) *Everywhere he goes the poor man has to work.*

22. **ADONDE VA EL VIOLIN va la bolsa.** (Wherever the violin goes the violin case has to go.) *Said of mothers who always chaperone their daughters.*

23. **A DONDE VA LA GENTE, va Vicente.** (Wherever the people go, Vincent goes.) *Monkey see, monkey do.*

24. **A FALTA DE PAN, buenas son 'cemitas.** (When there's

no white bread, brown bread will do.) *When we don't have what we like, we must like what we have.*

25. **AGARRA FAMA y échate en la cama.** (Acquire fame and go to bed.) *He who is famous may sleep 'til noon.*

26. **A GATO viejo, ratón tierno.** (To an old cat, a tender mouse.) *Censures old men who fall in love with young women.*

27. **AGUA ida no recogida.** (The water that's gone cannot be retrieved.) *What's done cannot be undone.*

28. **AGUA pasada no mueve molino.** (Water that's gone will not turn the mill.) *What's done cannot be undone.*

29. **AGUA que no has de beber, déjala correr.** (Water that you're not going to drink, let run.) *Don't be a dog in the manger.*

30. **AGUA revuelta ganancia de pescadores.** (Muddy waters are the fisherman's boon.) *People often take advantage of a situation in turmoil.*

31. **A HIERRO caliente, batir de repente.** (Iron must be hammered while it is still hot.) *Strike while the iron is hot.*

32. **AHORA ES EL REIR, después será el freír.** (Laugh now— the frying comes later.) *He laughs best who laughs last.*

33. **A JACAL viejo no le faltan goteras.** (An old hut is never without leaks.) *Old age is a series of ills.*

34. **A JUVENTUD ociosa, vejez trabajosa.** (An idle youth is followed by an old age full of hardships.) *Recommends hard work in one's youth.*

35. **A LA GUERRA con la guerra.** (Fight war with war.) *Fight fire with fire.*

36. **A LA MEJOR COCINERA se le *ajuma* la olla.** (Even the best cook blackens her pot.) *We all make mistakes.*

37. **AL AMIGO y al caballo, no cansarlos.** (Tire out neither your friend nor your horse.) *Friendship is not to be abused.*

38. **A LA MUJER, ni todo el amor, ni todo el dinero.** (Give

3

your wife neither all your love, nor all your money.) *Advises against spoiling one's wife.*

39. **A LA MUJER sola todos le dan con el pie.** (Everybody kicks a woman who is alone.) *A woman who is alone in the world is mistreated by everyone.*

40. **AL ARRIESGADO la suerte le da la mano.** (Fortune extends her hand to the daring man.) *Nothing ventured, nothing gained.*

41. **A LA VEJEZ, viruelas.** (The pox in old age.) *Censures old men who fall in love with young women.*

42. **AL BUEN CALLAR llaman Sancho.** (Honest silence is called Sancho.) *Silence is golden.*

43. **AL BUEN ENTENDEDOR, pocas palabras.** (For one who understands well, few words are sufficient.) *A word to the wise is sufficient.*

44. **AL BUEY por el cuerno y al hombre por la palabra.** (The ox is appraised by its horns, the man by his word.) *An honest man's word is as good as his bond.*

45. **ALCANZA quien no cansa.** (He achieves who doesn't tire out.) *He who perseveres goes far.*

46. **AL ENFERMO que es de vida, hasta 'l agua le es medicina.** (The patient who is destined to live can be cured even with water.) *God has the final say as to who is to live or die.*

47. **A LEPERO, lépero y medio.** (A rogue, after a rogue.) *Send out a thief to catch a thief.*

48. **AL FREIR será el reír.** (Laughing comes at frying time.) *He who laughs last laughs best.*

49. **ALGO TIENE ESTA AGUA porque la bendice el cura.** (There's something to this water, for the priest is blessing it.) *Uncalled-for praise gives rise to suspicion.*

50. **ALLA VAN LEYES do quieren reyes.** (Laws go wherever kings want them to go.) *The wishes of the powerful overcome justice and reason.*

51. **AL LOCO y al aire, darles calle.** (Clear the way for mad-

4

men and the wind.) *Recommends against getting into an argument with a stubborn, silly person.*

52. **AL MAL MUSICO hasta las uñas le estorban.** (A poor musician even has trouble with his fingernails.) *Some people are nothing but excuses when asked to do something.*

53. **AL MARRANO más trompudo le toca la mejor mazorca.** (The pig with the largest snout gets the choicest ear of corn.) *Said by people who are jealous of the luck of an aggressive man when they see him in the company of a beautiful woman.*

54. **AL MEJOR COCINERO se le va un tomate entero.** (Even the best cook lets a whole tomato go through.) *We all make mistakes.*

55. **AL MENTIROSO le conviene ser memorioso.** (It is convenient for a liar to have a good memory.) *A liar should have a good memory.*

56. **AL NOPAL lo van a ver sólo cuando tiene tunas.** (People seek the cactus only when they need prickly pears.) *Satirizes fair-weather friends.*

57. **A LO DADO, hasta los obispos trotan.** (Giving things away brings the bishops trotting.) *Suggests that when things are given away, people come running.*

58. **A LO DADO no se le busca lado.** (Don't look for defects in a gift.) *Don't look a gift horse in the mouth.*

59. **A LO HECHO, pecho.** (What's done must be faced.) *What's done cannot be undone.*

60. **A LO QUE te *truje*, Chencha.** (Let's do our thing, Chencha.) *A humorous expression meaning let's get down to business.*

61. **AL PERRO más flaco se le cargan las pulgas.** (The scrawniest dog gets the most fleas.) *When it rains, it pours.*

62. **AL QUE DA y quita le sale una jorobita.** (He who gives and claims back the gift grows a hump.) *Advises against giving something and then wanting it back.*

63. **AL QUE DIOS se la tiene, San Pedro se la bendiga.** (He whom God protects, St. Peter blesses.) *All the water runs to the mill of a lucky person.*

64. **AL QUE LE DUELE la muela, que se la saque.** (Let he who has the toothache have his tooth extracted.) *If the shoe fits, wear it.*

65. **AL QUE LE VENGA la bota, que se la ponga.** (If the boot fits, wear it.) *If the shoe fits, wear it.*

66. **AL QUE MADRUGA, Dios le ayuda.** (God helps an early riser.) *The early bird catches the worm.*

67. **AL QUE NACE pa panzón, aunque lo fajen de niño.** (He who is born to be fat will be so even though you bind him as a child.) *What is bred in the bone will never come out of the flesh.*

68. **AL QUE NACE pa tamal, del cielo le caen las hojas.** (He who is born to be a tamale gets his husks from heaven.) *Suggests that some people are naturally slow and dull.*

69. **AL QUE NO HA usado huaraches, las correas le sacan sangre.** (He who has never worn sandals is easily cut by the straps.) *It's hard to do things that one is not used to doing.*

70. **AL QUE POR SU GUSTO muere, hasta la muerte le sabe.** (He who dies of his own free will finds death sweet.) *He who wants to die even savors death.*

71. **AL QUE SE ALEJA lo olvidan y al que se muere lo entierran.** (He who goes away is forgotten, and he who dies is buried.) *Out of sight, out of mind.*

72. **AL QUE SE AYUDA, Dios le ayuda.** (God helps him who helps himself.) *God helps those that help themselves.*

73. **AL QUE TIENE CABALLADA le dan un potro y al que no tiene le quitan otro.** (He who has many horses is given a colt, and he who has none loses another one.) *The rich get richer, the poor get poorer.*

74. **AL TIEMPO de los higos, no hay amigos.** (When figs are ready to pick, there are no friends to help pick them.) *A comment on fair-weather friends.*

75. **AMA A TU PROJIMO como a ti mismo.** (Love your neighbor as you love yourself.) *Love thy neighbor as thyself.*

76. **A MACHO VIEJO, aparejo nuevo.** (An old mule deserves a new harness.) *Suggests making work easier for an old worker.*

77. **A MAL TIEMPO, buena cara.** (Face adversity with a good countenance.) *Recommends facing adversity cheerfully.*

78. **AMANTE ausentado, amante olvidado.** (The lover who is absent is soon forgotten.) *Out of sight, out of mind.*

79. **AMIGO en la adversidad, amigo de verdad.** (A friend in adversity is a true friend.) *A friend in need is a friend indeed.*

80. **AMIGO que no es cierto: con un ojo cerrado y el otro abierto.** (Watch a friend who is not constant with one eye shut and the other open.) *Don't trust an untried friend.*

81. **AMOR con amor se paga.** (Love is paid with love.) *One good turn deserves another.*

82. **AMOR de lejos es pa los pendejos.** (Love at a distance is for fools.) *Love from far away is for fools.*

83. **AMOR, dinero, y cuidados no pueden ser disimulados.** (Love, money, and care cannot be feigned.) *Riches and one's feelings are hard to hide.*

84. **AMOR que ha sido brasa de repente vuelve a arder.** (A love that still flickers can easily reignite.) *Where there's smoke, there's fire.*

85. **AMOR viejo, ni te olvido ni te dejo.** (Old love, I can neither forget you nor give you up.) *An old love is never forgotten.*

86. **AMOR y aborrecimiento no quitan conocimiento.** (Love and hatred have nothing to do with reasoning.) *Advice against being partial.*

87. **A MUELE y muele ni metate queda.** (Persistent grinding wears away the grinding stone.) *He who perseveres goes far.*

88. **ANDA AL AS y ganarás.** (Bet on the ace and you will win.) *Suggests betting on sure things.*

89. **ANIMALES ingratos: las mujeres y los gatos.** (Women and cats are ungrateful animals.) *A comment on the ungratefulness of women.*

90. **ANTES QUE ACABES, no te alabes.** (Don't praise yourself before you finish.) *Don't whistle until you're out of the woods.*

91. **ANTES QUE TE CASES, mira lo que haces.** (Before you marry, consider what you're doing.) *Look before you leap.*

92. **ANTES SON MIS DIENTES que mis parientes.** (My teeth come before my relatives.) *After me, you are next.*

93. **A PADRE allegador, hijo expendedor.** (For a frugal father, a spendthrift son.) *After a gatherer comes a scatterer.*

94. **A PALABRAS locas, oídos sordos.** (Deaf ears to foolish words.) *Foolish questions deserve no answer.*

95. **A PALABRAS necias, oídos sordos.** (Turn deaf ears to foolish words.) *Foolish questions deserve no answer.*

96. **A PAN DURO, diente agudo.** (Stale bread calls for sharp teeth.) *No gains without pains.*

97. **A PERRO viejo no hay cuz, cuz.** (You can't get close to an old dog by calling out *cuz, cuz*.) *There is no catching old birds with chaff.*

98. **A PERRO viejo todo son pulgas.** (To an old dog, everything's fleas.) *Old age is a series of ills.*

99. **A PLATO lleno lo colman.** (A full plate is filled over.) *Them that has, gits.*

100. **APRENDIZ de todo, oficial de nada.** (Apprentice of all trades, master of none.) *Jack of all trades, master of none.*

101. **APURATE DESPACIO.** (Hurry up slowly.) *Make haste slowly.*

102. **AQUEL QUE MAS ALTO SUBE, más grande porrazo da.** (He who climbs highest has the hardest fall.) *The bigger they are, the harder they fall.*

103. **AQUEL QUE NO OYE CONSEJO nunca a viejo llegará.** (He who doesn't listen to advice will never become old.) *Suggests listening to advice.*

104. **AQUELLOS SON RICOS que tienen amigos.** (Rich are they who have friends.) *When there are friends, there is wealth.*

105. **A QUIEN DIOS no le da hijos, el diablo le da sobrinos.** (He to whom God gives no children, the devil gives nephews.) *A person with no obligations often gets those of his friends.*

106. **A QUIEN DIOS quiere bien, uvas le da el laurel.** (He whom God loves, reaps grapes from the laurel shrub.) *Where God's blessings dwell, prosperity follows.*

107. **A QUIEN DIOS se la diere, San Pedro se la bendiga.** (He whom God chooses to give a thing, St. Peter shall bless.) *One must be resigned to one's lot.*

108. **A QUIEN LE DAN no escoge.** (He who receives a gift can't be choosy.) *Beggars can't be choosers.*

109. **¡A QUIEN LE DAN pan que llore!** (Who will cry if he's given bread!) *What better fare than well content?*

110. **A QUIEN MADRUGA, Dios le ayuda.** (God helps an early riser.) *Recommends constant work in order to prosper.*

111. **A QUIEN NO HABLA, Dios no lo oye.** (God does not hear those who don't speak up.) *God helps those that help themselves.*

112. **ARBOL que crece torcido nunca su tronco endereza.** (The tree that grows crooked will never straighten its trunk.) *As the twig is bent, so will the tree grow.*

113. **ARMAS y dinero buenas manos quieren.** (Firearms and money call for good hands.) *Warns that firearms and money should be handled responsibly.*

114. **ARRIERO que vende mula, o tira coz o recula.** (The muleteer who sells his mule does so either because it kicks or because it rears.) *Warns against being duped by buying defective items.*

115. **ARRIEROS somos y en el camino andamos.** (We are muleteers and travel the highroads.) *Warns that people can and will get even for any wrong done to them.*

116. **ARRIMATE A LOS BUENOS y serás uno de ellos.** (Keep company with good people and you will be one of them.) *Suggests that you are judged by the company you keep.*

117. **ARROZ que no se menea se quema.** (The rice that is not stirred will burn.) *Don't let the grass grow under your feet.*

118. **A TI TE LO DIGO, mi hija, pero entiéndelo tú, mi nuera.** (I'm telling you, my daughter, but it is meant for you, my daughter-in-law.) *People should take a hint.*

119. **A TODO GUAJOLOTITO se le llega su Noche Buena.** (Every little turkey has his Christmas Eve.) *Every dog has his day.*

120. **A TU TIERRA, grulla, que ésta no es tuya.** (Go home, crane, this is not your land.) *People are often better off among their own folks than with strangers.*

121. **A UN ENTREMETIDO nunca le va bien.** (A meddler never fares well.) *Suggests that things don't go well for a meddler.*

122. **AUNQUE LA MONA se vista de seda, mona se queda.** (Even though the monkey dresses in silk, it's still a monkey.) *Dress a monkey as you will, it remains a monkey still.*

123. **AUNQUE TE DIGAN que sí, espérate a que lo veas.** (Even though they may tell you that it is so, wait until you see it.) *To believe with certainty, one must begin by doubting.*

124. **AUNQUE TODOS SOMOS del mismo barro, no es lo mismo bacín que jarro.** (Even though we are made of the same clay, there's a difference between a chamber pot and a pitcher.) *Censures people for not knowing their place.*

125. **AYUDATE que Dios te ayudará.** (Help yourself, for God will help you.) *God helps those that help themselves.*

Barriga llena, corazón contento.
A full belly, a happy heart.

126. **BAILE Y COCHINO, en la casa del vecino.** (A dance and a pig, in the neighbor's house.) *Suggests that one stay away from inconveniences.*

127. **BAJO LA BARBA CANA, vive la mujer honrada.** (Under a gray beard lives an honorable woman.) *The respectability of an older man gives his wife protection.*

128. **BAJO LA DESCONFIANZA vive la seguridad.** (Beneath mistrust lives security.) *Suggests that to live securely one not trust just anybody.*

129. **BALA QUE ZUMBA no mata.** (A zooming bullet seldom kills.) *Great talkers are little doers.*

130. **BARCO que mandan muchos pilotos pronto se va a pique.** (A ship with many skippers soon sinks.) *Too many cooks spoil the broth.*

131. **BARRIGA LLENA, corazón contento.** (A full belly, a happy heart.) *Contentment begins in one's stomach.*

132. **BELLEZA y hermosura, poco duran.** (Loveliness and beauty are short lived.) *Beauty is fleeting.*

133. **BIEN CANTA MARTA, después de harta.** (Martha sings well on a full stomach.) *A person is happy after achieving some particular end.*

11

134. **BIEN PREDICA quien bien vive.** (He preaches well who lives well.) *Practice what you preach.*

135. **BIEN REZA pero mal ofrece.** (He prays well but offers poorly.) *It's easier said than done.*

136. **BIEN SABE EL BURRO en qué casa rebuzna.** (The donkey knows well in whose house he brays.) *Censures those who take advantage of a person's kindness.*

137. **BIEN SABE EL DIABLO a quién se le aparece.** (The devil knows well whom he can frighten.) *Some people take advantage of those who cannot fight back.*

138. **BIEN TRAJADO, bien mirado.** (Well dressed, rightly admired.) *Clothes make the man.*

139. **BIEN VENGAS, MAL, si vienes solo.** (Welcome, misfortune, if you come alone.) *Misfortunes never come singly.*

140. **BIENVENIDOS LOS HUESPEDES por el gusto que dan, cuando se van.** (Guests are welcome for the joy they bring, when they depart.) *Recommends short visits.*

141. **BOCA DE MIEL, manos de hiel.** (Mouth of honey, hands of bile.) *A saint's words, a cat's paws.*

142. **BOLSA SIN DINERO, llámola cuero.** (An empty purse I call rawhide.) *The value of the purse is the money it contains.*

143. **BUEN ABOGADO, mal vecino.** (Good lawyer, bad neighbor.) *Good lawyers make bad neighbors.*

144. **BUEN ARRIERO, la cama tiende primero.** (The good muleteer makes his bed first.) *Forewarned is forearmed.*

145. **BUENAS SON MANGAS después de Pascuas.** (Conveniences are fine even if after Easter.) *Better late than never.*

146. **BUENAS SON MIS VECINAS, pero me faltan tres gallinas.** (My neighbors are nice but I'm missing three chickens.) *You can't judge a book by its cover.*

147. **BUENA VIDA, arrugas trae.** (A good life brings wrinkles.) *Those who live well live long.*

148. BUENA VIDA, padre y madre olvida. (A good life makes us forget our parents.) *Suggests that if times are good, parents are taken for granted.*

149. BUENO ES CULANTRO, pero no tanto. (Coriander is good, but not in excess.) *Too much of a good thing is not good.*

150. BUEN VESTIDO y limpieza no andan con pobreza. (A fine dress and cleanliness do not keep company with poverty.) *Good clothes and neatness are a luxury to the poor.*

151. BUEY VIEJO, surco derecho. (An old ox, a straight furrow.) *An experienced person does the best work.*

152. BURRO CHIQUITO, siempre mocito. (The small donkey always looks young.) *Small people do not seem to age.*

153. BURRO de muchos amos se lo comen los animales. (A donkey owned by many is eaten by the animals.) *Everybody's business is nobody's business.*

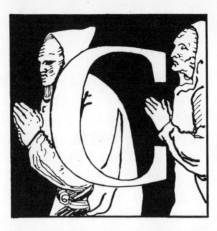

Con la boca adorando y con el mazo dando.
Praying devoutly but hammering stoutly.

154. **CABALLO alazán tostado, primero muerto que cansado.** (A sorrel-colored horse would rather die than show fatigue.) *A comment on the stamina of a sorrel-colored horse.*

155. **CABALLO al caballero, para el mulato mula y para el indio burra.** (A horse for the gentleman, a mule for the mulatto, and a burro for the Indian.) *A discriminatory comment.*

156. **CABALLO matado siempre se pandea.** (A horse with a sore on his back will always flinch.) *People are sensitive to the mention of their defects.*

157. **CABALLO que vuela no quiere espuela.** (A fast horse does not need a spur.) *Never spur a willing horse.*

158. **CADA CABEZA es un mundo.** (Each head is a world.) *So many heads, so many worlds.*

159. **CADA chango a su mecate.** (Each monkey to his own swing.) *Said when everybody is busy doing some particular task.*

160. **CADA cosa se parece a su dueño.** (Everything resembles its owner.) *Like father, like son.*

161. **CADA cual es hijo de sus obras.** (Each one is the son of his works.) *A man is known by his works.*

162. **CADA CUBETA huele a lo que tiene dentro.** (Each bucket smells of its contents.) *A person's character shows in his actions.*

163. **CADA LOCO con su tema (y yo con mi terquedad).** (Each madman to his own madness [and I with my stubbornness]). *Said when everyone is busy doing some particular task.*

164. **CADA MAESTRITO tiene su librito.** (Each little schoolmaster has his favorite little book.) *Everyone has his own particular way of doing things.*

165. **CADA OVEJA con su pareja.** (Every sheep with its kind.) *Birds of a feather flock together.*

166. **CADA PERRO tiene su garrote.** (Every dog has his cudgel.) *Every dog has his day.*

167. **CADA quien con su cada cual.** (Each one with his equal.) *Like seeks like.*

168. **CADA quien es dueño de su miedo.** (Each one is the owner of his fear.) *Satiric comment on those who show fear.*

169. **CADA quien sabe dónde le aprieta el zapato.** (Each one knows where his shoe pinches.) *Everyone knows his own worries and sorrows.*

170. **CADA quien sabe lo que lleva su costal.** (Each one knows what his bag is carrying.) *Everyone knows what his worries and sorrows are.*

171. **CADA quien se rasca con sus uñas.** (Everyone scratches himself with his own fingernails.) *Each one's business is his business.*

172. **CADA quien siente su mal.** (Each one feels his own misfortune.) *Each one knows where his shoe pinches.*

173. **CADA quien tiene su modo de dar chiche.** (Each one has her own way of breast feeding.) *Everyone has his or her own particular way of doing things.*

15

174. CADA SANTO elogia su parroquia. (Each saint praises his own parish.) *People tend to praise their own things even when they know they have little merit.*

175. CADA SANTO quiere su candela. (Every saint wants his own candle.) *Give to others their due and respect them.*

176. CADA SEMANA tiene su día santo. (Each week has its holiday.) *All things have their good and bad qualities.*

177. CADA UNO *destornuda* como Dios le ayuda. (Everyone sneezes as God helps him.) *Everyone does his work as best he can or knows how.*

178. CADA UNO en su casa y Dios en la de todos. (Everyone in his own home and God in everyone's.) *Suggests not interfering in other people's affairs.*

179. CADA UNO extiende la pierna hasta donde alcanza la cobija. (Everyone stretches his leg as far as the blanket reaches.) *We all adapt ourselves to a given situation.*

180. CADA UNO habla de la feria *asegún* le va en ella. (Everyone talks about the fair according to how he fares there.) *Everyone has a right to his own opinion.*

181. CADA UNO *jala* pa su lado. (Each one pulls in his own direction.) *Everyone looks after his own interests.*

182. CADA UNO sabe dónde le aprieta el zapato. (Everyone knows where the shoe pinches.) *Everyone knows what is best for his own convenience, health, and comfort.*

183. CADA UNO siente su mal. (Everyone feels his own misfortune.) *Everyone knows where his shoe pinches.*

184. CADA VIEJITO alaba su bordoncito. (Each little old man praises his cane.) *Everyone praises what is his, regardless of its merit.*

185. CAE MAS PRONTO un hablador que un cojo. (A liar falls faster than a lame man.) *Liars are easily found out.*

186. CALABAZA caliente, pedo de repente. (Hot pumpkin, sudden flatulence.) *Advice against eating hot pumpkin.*

187. CALLE EL QUE DIO y hable el que tomó. (He who gave

should keep silent; he who received should talk.) *He who gives should not boast; he who receives should be thankful.*

188. **CALLE PASAJERA no cría hierba.** (A busy street grows no weeds.) *Don't let the grass grow under your feet.*

189. **CAMBIO de pasto engorda la ternera.** (A change of pasture fattens the calf.) *Changes of environment are good for one's well being.*

190. **CANA engaña, diente miente, arruga desengaña.** (Gray hair deceives, teeth lie, but wrinkles tell the tale.) *A comment on how wrinkles show one's age.*

191. **CANDIL de la calle y oscuridad de su casa.** (A lamp in the street and darkness at home.) *Charity begins at home.*

192. **CARA de santo, uñas de gato.** (Face of a saint and claws of a cat.) *Said of people who pretend to be righteous.*

193. **CARA vemos, corazón no sabemos.** (Face we see, heart we know not.) *Appearances are deceiving.*

194. **CARGADO de fierro, cargado de miedo.** (Armed with guns, weighed down by fear.) *He who is heavily armed must have great fears.*

195. **CASADO, pero no capado.** (Married, yes, but not castrated.) *Said by married men who are asked why they are stepping out on their wives.*

196. **CASA empeñada, pobre y desamparada.** (A mortgaged house looks poor and forsaken.) *People lose interest in a home that is mortgaged.*

197. **CASAMIENTO de pobres, fábrica de limosneros.** (A marriage between two poor people is a factory of beggars.) *Counsels against two poor persons marrying.*

198. **CASAMIENTO dilatado, mal hecho y desbaratado.** (A postponed marriage is badly made and often broken up.) *Recommends that a marriage be arranged promptly.*

199. **CASA puerca, gente espera.** (An unkept house expects guests.) *Guests seem to drop in when the house is dirtiest.*

200. CAYO LA *SOPA* en la miel. (The bread pudding fell in the honey.) *Said when a person gets a windfall.*

201. CEDACITO nuevo, buen cernidor. (A new sieve sifts well.) *People take care of things while the novelty lasts.*

202. COME PAN y bebe agua y vivirás larga vida. (Eat bread and drink water and you will live long.) *A person lives longer if he eats with moderation.*

203. COMER y rascar, todo es comenzar. (Eating and scratching need but a start.) *Said when someone is reluctant to get started on some task.*

204. COME y bebe, que la vida es breve. (Eat and drink, for life is short.) *Eat, drink, and be merry, for tomorrow we die.*

205. COMIDA hecha, compañía deshecha. (The meal over, the company disappears.) *Censures those whose friendship lasts only while they are receiving some benefit.*

206. COMO DUEÑO de mi atole, lo menearé con un palo. (As the owner of my gruel, I'll stir it with a stick.) *Suggests that people can do whatever they want with their own things.*

207. COMO EL PERRO del hortelano, que ni come ni deja comer al amo. (Like the dog in the manger, who neither eats nor lets his master eat.) *Don't be a dog in the manger.*

208. COMO ES EL SAPO es la pedrada. (As the toad is, so is the blow with the stone.) *Suggests that the effort is as important as the end desired.*

209. COMO ES LA VIDA, así es la muerte. (As life is, so is death.) *As your days are spent, so shall they end.*

210. COMO HAY UNOS, hay otros. (Just as there is one, there are others.) *There is always someone better than you.*

211. COMO SE VIENE, se va. (As it comes, so it goes.) *Easy come, easy go.*

212. COMO SIEMBRAS, segarás. (As you plant, you will harvest.) *As you sow, so shall you reap.*

213. **COMO SU CARA, sus hechos.** (As his face is, so are his deeds.) *One's face betrays one's deeds.*

214. **COMO TE VEN, así te tratan.** (As they see you, so shall they treat you.) *Clothes make the man.*

215. **COMPADRE que a la comadre no le anda por las caderas, no es amigo de veras.** (The friend who doesn't make passes at one's wife is really not a friend.) *Hints that one's friends often make passes at a man's wife.*

216. **COMPAÑIA de dos, *compañía* de Dios.** (Company between two, company with God.) *Two's company, three's a crowd.*

217. **COMPUESTA, no hay mujer fea.** (Made up, there is no ugly woman.) *No woman is ugly when she's all made up.*

218. **CON AMOR y aguardiente, nada se siente.** (With love and brandy, nothing is felt.) *People in love or drunk are not conscious of others.*

219. **CON CRIOLLO civilizado, vete con cuidado.** (With a civilized *criollo*, tread carefully.) *Shows mistrust of Spaniards born in America.*

220. **CON DESEOS no se hacen templos.** (Temples are not built with wishes.) *It takes hard work to get ahead.*

221. **CONDICIONES rompen leyes.** (Circumstances break laws.) *Circumstances alter cases.*

222. **CON DINERO no se olvidan los encargos.** (No orders are forgotten when money is given.) *Censures those who ask friends to buy them things without giving them money.*

223. **CON DOS que se quieren bien, con uno que coma basta.** (Of two people in love, it's enough for only one to eat.) *Said of selfish persons who eat all they can without thinking of others.*

224. **CON EL TIEMPO se maduran las verdes.** (In time green fruit ripens.) *One must have patience to attain an end.*

225. **CON EL TIEMPO Y UN GANCHITO, hasta las verdes**

19

se alcanzan. (With time and a small hook, even the green ones can be reached.) *If one has patience, even the seemingly inaccessible can be attained.*

226. **CON LA BOCA adorando y con el mazo dando.** (Praying devoutly but hammering stoutly.) *Depend on others but mostly on yourself.*

227. **CON LAS GLORIAS se olvidan las memorias.** (When honors come, memories fade.) *Those who succeed are apt to forget friends and favors.*

228. **CON LAS QUE REPICAN, doblan.** (The same bells that ring, also toll.) *An eye for an eye and a tooth for a tooth.*

229. **CON LA VARA que midas serás medido.** (With the yardstick with which you measure others, you will be measured.) *Do unto others as you would have them do unto you.*

230. **CON LO MIO me ayude Dios.** (With my things, may God help me.) *Live and let live.*

231. **CON LO QUE NO CUESTA, se hace fiesta.** (With something that doesn't cost, one makes merry.) *One celebrates with fewer precautions when using someone else's possessions.*

232. **CON LO QUE SANA SUSANA cae enferma Juana.** (What cures Susan makes Jane ill.) *One man's food is another man's poison.*

233. **CON LOS AÑOS vienen los desengaños.** (With years come disillusionment.) *As the years pass, one sees things more as they are.*

234. **CON LOS CURAS y los gatos, pocos tratos.** (Have little to do with priests and cats.) *Advice against expecting too much from priests and cats.*

235. **CONOCEN A SAN DAME pero a San Toma no.** (They know St. Give but not St. Take.) *Censures persons who are willing to accept gifts but never give anything in return.*

236. **CON PACIENCIA se comió el piojo a la pulga.** (With patience the louse ate the flea.) *It takes patience to achieve one's goals.*

20

237. **CON PACIENCIA se gana el cielo.** (Heaven is gained with patience.) *Patience is its own reward.*

238. **CON PACIENCIA se gana la gloria.** (Heaven is gained with patience.) *Patience is its own reward.*

239. **CON TARUGO ni a misa porque se voltea pal coro.** (With the stupid I wouldn't even go to mass, because they turn toward the choir [with their backs to the altar].) *Suggests that we be selective in the company we keep.*

240. **CONTIGO, pan y cebolla.** (With you, bread and onions.) *Two can live as cheaply as one.*

241. **CONTRA AMOR y fortuna no hay defensa alguna.** (There is no defense against love and fate.) *Love always finds a way.*

242. **CON TRAJE de baño, no hay engaño.** (There is no deceiving in a bathing suit.) *One's physique cannot be hidden in a bathing suit.*

243. **CON VIRTUD y bondad se adquiere autoridad.** (With virtue and goodness one acquires authority.) *Authority is gained through virtue and kindness.*

244. **CORTESIA de boca, mucho consigue y nada cuesta.** (Lip service attains a great deal and costs nothing.) *Being courteous doesn't cost anything.*

245. **COSA mala nunca muere.** (An evil thing never dies.) *A bad penny always comes back.*

246. **COSA platicada, mal hecha y desbaratada.** (A thing that's discussed will be badly done and finally ruined.) *A warning not to discuss your plans.*

247. **COSAS A DIOS dejadas son bien vengadas.** (Things left to God are well avenged.) *Leave revenge to God.*

248. **COSTUMBRES y dinero hacen a los hijos caballeros.** (Customs and money make our children into gentlemen.) *Manners and money make gentlemen out of young men.*

249. **CREE EL LADRON que todos son de su condición.** (The thief thinks everyone's a thief.) *Like suspects like.*

250. CRIA CUERVOS y te sacarán los ojos. (Raise crows and they will pluck out your eyes.) *Suggests not raising a viper in one's bosom.*

251. CRIA FAMA y échate en la cama. (Acquire fame and lie down in bed.) *He who has the fame of an early riser can sleep 'til noon.*

252. CUANDO DICEN TOMA, hasta el rey se asoma. (When it's a question of giving things away, even the king looks out of the window.) *Don't look a gift horse in the mouth.*

253. CUANDO DIOS amanece, para todos aparece. (When God rises, He rises for all men.) *When God dawns, He appears for all.*

254. CUANDO DIOS da, da a manos llenas. (When God gives, He gives abundantly.) *God does not stint on His bounties.*

255. CUANDO DIOS no quiere, santo no puede. (When God is not willing, the saint cannot make the miracle.) *A saint cannot, if God will not.*

256. CUANDO DIOS quiere, 'l agua es medecina. (When God wills it, even water is medicine.) *God's will is all that's necessary.*

257. CUANDO EL COYOTE predica no están seguros los pobres. (When the coyote preaches the poor are not safe.) *Beware of Greeks bearing gifts.*

258. CUANDO EL DIABLO reza, engañar quiere. (When the devil prays, he wants to deceive.) *Too much courtesy, too much craft.*

259. CUANDO EL DINERO habla, todos callan. (When money talks, everyone shuts up.) *Money talks.*

260. CUANDO EL GATO no está en casa, los ratones se pasean. (When the cat's not at home, the mice go visiting.) *When the cat's away, the mice will play.*

261. CUANDO EL INDIO encanece, el español no parece. (When the Indian gets gray hair, the Spaniard is dead.) *Comments on life expectancy between Indian and Spaniard.*

262. **CUANDO EL MAL no tiene cura, nomás morirse es remedio.** (When there is no cure for an illness, the best remedy is death.) *There are things that cannot be helped, regardless of efforts to the contrary.*

263. **CUANDO EL RIO suena, agua lleva.** (When the river makes noise, it is carrying water.) *Most rumors have some foundation.*

264. **CUANDO EL SARTEN chilla, algo hay en la villa.** (When the frying pan sizzles, something's up in the village.) *Most rumors have some foundation.*

265. **CUANDO EL SOL sale, para todos sale.** (When the sun rises it rises for everyone.) *God showers His blessings on all alike.*

266. **CUANDO ESTES EN LA ABUNDANCIA, acuérdate de la calamidad.** (When there is abundance, remember calamity.) *Forget not adversity in times of prosperity.*

267. **CUANDO HAY SANTOS nuevos, los viejos no hacen milagros.** (When there are new saints, the old ones do not perform any new miracles.) *Things are all right when they are new or until the novelty wears off.*

268. **CUANDO LA PARTERA es mala le echa la culpa al chamaco.** (When the midwife is inefficient she blames the newborn.) *Said of people who are always giving excuses for their shortcomings.*

269. **CUANDO LA PUERCA lava, el cielo se le nubla.** (When the untidy woman washes, the sky clouds up.) *Dirty people always have excuses to be dirty.*

270. **CUANDO LA VACA es ligera, la ternera va adelante.** (When the cow is fast the heifer is even faster.) *Implies that a child will exceed the pace set by the parent.*

271. **CUANDO LLUEVE y hace viento, quédate adentro.** (When it rains and is windy, stay indoors.) *Advises one to avoid getting in trouble.*

272. **CUANDO NO HAY CARNE de lomo, de toda como.** (When there's no sirloin, I'll eat any meat.) *Beggars can't be choosers.*

23

273. **CUANDO NO HAY PAN, buenas son 'cemitas.** (When there's no bread, sweet rolls will do.) *When we don't have what we like, we must like what we have.*

274. **CUANDO SE DICE TOMA, hasta el rey se asoma.** (When things are being given away, even the king takes a look.) *You don't look a gift horse in the mouth.*

275. **CUANDO SE ENOJAN LAS COMADRES, se dicen las verdades.** (When women friends quarrel, they become truthful.) *When women friends quarrel, they tell each other things they wouldn't otherwise.*

276. **CUANDO SE REVUELVE 'l agua, cualquier ajolote es bagre.** (When the water is muddy, any water dog is a catfish.) *When changes in social order come, moral values are confused.*

277. **CUANDO TE COMPREN, vende, y cuando te vendan, compra.** (When you have a buyer, sell; when people need to sell, buy.) *Advises one to avail oneself of all opportunities.*

278. **CUANDO TE DEN LA TERNERA, acude con el *cabresto*.** (When they give you the heifer, make haste to bring the rope.) *Opportunity knocks but once.*

279. **CUANDO TOMA CUERPO, EL DIABLO se disfraza de abogado.** (When the devil assumes human form, he disguises himself as a lawyer.) *A belief that lawyers are evil.*

280. **CUANDO UNA PUERTA se cierra, cien se abren.** (When one door closes, a hundred open.) *Recommends that one never lose hope of something's turning up.*

281. **CUANDO UN CUBO sube, otro baja.** (When one bucket goes up, another comes down.) *Life has its ups and downs.*

282. **CUANDO VAYAS A CASA ajena, llama a la puerta.** (When you go to someone else's home, knock at the door.) *Warns one not to be too familiar in others' homes.*

283. **CUANDO VEN UN POBRE *CAIDO* todos le dan con el pie.** (When people see a poor man down, everyone kicks

24

him.) *People kick a man when he's down.*

284. CUANTO más aprisa, menos adelante. (The faster one goes, the less progress one makes.) *Haste makes waste.*

285. CUIDA TU CASA y deja la ajena. (Take care of your home and leave the other fellow's alone.) *Advises one to mind one's own business.*

286. CUIDA TUS CENTAVOS y los pesos se cuidarán solos. (Take care of your pennies and the dollars will take care of themselves.) *Advises one to be frugal.*

De donde relampaguea, de allí ventea.
Where there's lightning there's wind.

287. **DA MAS EL DURO que el desnudo.** (The miser has more to give than the destitute.) *You can't get blood out of a turnip.*

288. **DAME DONDE ME SIENTE, que yo veré donde me acueste.** (Give me a place to sit down and I'll find a place to lie down.) *Give some people an inch and they'll take a mile.*

289. **DAR UNA EN EL CLAVO y dos en la herradura.** (To hit once on the nail and twice on the horseshoe.) *To do a thing right by accident or chance.*

290. **DAR Y QUITAR: pecado mortal.** (To give and take is a mortal sin.) *Advice against giving something then wanting it returned.*

291. **DATE BUENA VIDA, sentirás más la caída.** (Lead a pampered life and you will feel the fall hardest.) *Warns against a life of ease in one's youth in the face of an uncertain life of hardship in old age.*

292. **DA Y TEN, y harás bien.** (Give and retain and you will do all right.) *Be liberal but prudent.*

293. **DE AFUERA vendrá el que de tu casa te echará.** (From outside will come someone who drives you from your

home.) *Rebukes those who start giving orders in others'*
homes.

294. **DE AMOR Y AMOR, sólo amor.** (From love and love,
only love.) *Only love is given away freely.*

295. **DE ARDOR mueren los quemados (y de frío los encuerados).** (Those who get burned die of the burning pain
[and the destitute freeze to death].) *Rebukes those persons who feel envious of others' receiving some benefit.*

296. **DE BAJADA hasta las piedras ruedan.** (Downhill even
stones roll downward.) *It takes no hard work to do an
easy task.*

297. **DE CARROCERO bajó a perrero.** (From coach maker
down to dog catcher.) *From driver down to dog catcher.*

298. **DE CRISTO a Cristo el más apolillado se raja.** (Of two
crucifixes, the one that's more moth-eaten will crack.)
*Of two good men, the one with less stamina will back
down.*

299. **DE CUERO AJENO, correas largas.** (From someone
else's rawhide, one makes the longest thongs.) *Censures
those who are most liberal with other people's things.*

300. **DE DECIR y hacer hay mucho que ver.** (There's much
to do between saying and doing.) *It's easier said than
done.*

301. **DE DINEROS y bondad, siempre la mitad.** (Of money
and kindness, always half.) *Don't be too liberal with
your money or your help.*

302. **DE DIOS viene el bien y de las abejas la miel.** (Goodness
comes from God as honey comes from bees.) *Blessings
come from God through whatever means they may come.*

303. **DE DONDE RELAMPAGUEA, de allí ventea.** (Where
there's lightning, there's wind.) *Where there's smoke,
there's fire.*

304. **DE DOS MALES, el menor.** (Of two evils, the lesser.)
Choose the lesser of two evils.

305. **DE DOS que se quieren mucho, con uno que coma basta.**
(Between two people who love each other dearly, if one

eats it is sufficient.) *Rebukes those who take advantage of some benefit that could be shared by others.*

306. **DE ESA TOGA murió mi gato.** (My cat died from the same arrogance.) *Advice against being arrogant.*

307. **DE ESCARMENTADOS se hacen los avisados.** (From the experienced come the cautious.) *Experience is a great teacher.*

308. **DE FAVOR te abrazan y quieres que te aprieten.** (They put their arms around you only as a favor, and you want them to hug you tightly.) *Give you an inch and you'll take a mile.*

309. **DE GOLOSOS y tragones están llenos los panteones.** (Cemeteries are full of gluttons and heavy drinkers.) *Chides those who eat or drink excessively.*

310. **DE GRANO en grano llena la gallina el buche.** (Grain by grain the hen fills her crop.) *Penny by penny saved up will be many.*

311. **DE GUSTOS no hay nada escrito.** (There's nothing written on tastes.) *Everyone to his taste.*

312. **DE HORA a hora, Dios mejora.** (From hour to hour, God improves one's health.) *Heaven sends help when the time is ripe.*

313. **DE LA ABUNDANCIA del corazón habla la boca.** (The mouth speaks from the abundance of the heart.) *The kind and noble of heart judge others kindly.*

314. **DEL AGUA mansa líbreme Dios.** (God protect me from still water.) *Beware of a silent dog and still water.*

315. **DE LA MANO a la boca se pierde la sopa.** (From the hand to the mouth the soup is lost.) *There's many a slip 'twixt the cup and the lip.*

316. **DE LA MUERTE y de la suerte no hay quien se escape.** (From death and fate no one escapes.) *There's no escaping fate or death.*

317. **DEL ARBOL *caído* todos hacen leña.** (Everyone makes firewood from a fallen tree.) *Chides those who kick a man when he's down.*

318. **DE LAS MUJERES bonitas se hacen los enamorados.** (Beautiful women give rise to lovers.) *Without beautiful women there wouldn't be any lovers.*

319. **DE LAS NUEVE en adelante no hay visita que se aguante.** (From nine o'clock on, no guest is welcome.) *Don't overstay your welcome.*

320. **DE LAS RODILLAS para abajo, todo son corvas.** (From the knees down it's all hams.) *Said of or to persons who show fear.*

321. **DE LA SUERTE y de la muerte no hay quien se escape.** (From fate and death no one escapes.) *There's no escaping fate or death.*

322. **DEL CIELO a la tierra no hay nada oculto.** (From heaven to earth there's nothing hidden.) *In time everything is found out.*

323. **DEL DATIL, hasta la palma.** (From the date to the palm.) *You don't look a gift horse in the mouth.*

324. **DEL DICHO al hecho hay mucho trecho.** (There's quite a gap between what is said and what is done.) *It's easier said than done.*

325. **DE LO CONTADO come el lobo.** (The wolf eats from what is told.) *Don't count your chickens before they're hatched.*

326. **DE LO DICHO a lo hecho hay un gran trecho.** (There's quite a gap between what is said and what is done.) *It's easier said than done.*

327. **DE LO PERDIDO, lo que parezca.** (Of what was lost, whatever turns up.) *Be content to recover whatever you can from a loss.*

328. **DE LOS PARIENTES y el sol, entre más lejos, mejor.** (Relatives and the sun, the farther away, the better.) *Suggests not getting too close to one's relatives.*

329. **DEL PALO *caido* todos hacen leña.** (Everyone makes firewood from a fallen tree.) *Chides those who kick a man when he's down.*

29

330. **DEL VIEJO, el consejo.** (Advice comes from the old.) *Experience gives advice.*

331. **DE MAÑANA en mañana bien pierde la oveja la lana.** (From day to day the sheep easily loses her wool.) *Don't put off for tomorrow what you can do today.*

332. **DE MEDICO, poeta, y loco, todos tenemos un poco.** (We all have in us a little of the physician, the poet, and the madman.) *It is normal for people to be helpful, feel poetic, and do crazy things from time to time.*

333. **DE MORIR yo y que se muera mi agüela, que se muera mi agüela que es más viejita.** (Between my grandmother's and my dying, let my grandmother die because she's older.) *A feeling that death can come for the other fellow but never for us.*

334. **DE MUCHOS CABITOS se hace un cirio pascual.** (Many small candle ends make a large candle.) *Little gains make a heavy purse.*

335. **DE NOCHE todos los gatos son pardos.** (All cats are gray at night.) *All women are fair when the candles are out.*

336. **DE PADRE cojo, hijo rengo.** (Lame father, lame son.) *Like father, like son.*

337. **DE PADRE santo, hijo diablo.** (From a good father, a bad son.) *Good education and training can do little with an evil nature.*

338. **DE PUERTA cerrada el diablo *juye*.** (The devil flees from a closed door.) *Lock your door and keep your neighbor honest.*

339. **DE QUE LOS HAY, los hay (la gracia es dar con ellos).** (That they exist there's no doubt [the thing is to find them].) *Said of persons who are easily exploited.*

340. **DE QUE SE MUERA mi padre y morirme yo, que se muera mi padre que es más viejo.** (Between my father's and my dying, let my father die because he is older.) *A feeling that death can come for the other fellow but never for us.*

341. **DESNUDA UN SANTO para vestir otro.** (Undress one

saint in order to dress another.) *Rob Peter to pay Paul.*

342. **DESPACIO, pero seguro.** (Slow, but sure.) *Patience is a virtue.*

343. **DESPACIO se llega a tiempo.** (Slowly, one arrives on time.) *Easy does it.*

344. **DESPACIO voy porque de prisa estoy.** (I am going slowly because I am in a hurry.) *Haste makes waste.*

345. **DESPUES DE COMER, ni un sobre escrito leer.** (After eating, read not even an envelope.) *Recommends not taxing one's eyes immediately after a meal.*

346. **DESPUES DE CONEJO ido, pedradas al matorral.** (After the rabbit's gone, they throw stones at the brush.) *Closing the barn door after the horse is stolen.*

347. **DESPUES DE CUERNOS, palos.** (After making a cuckold out of you, they beat you.) *Adding insult to injury.*

348. **DESPUES DEL ANIMAL robado, cerrar la puerta.** (After the animal is stolen, close the door.) *Closing the barn door after the horse is stolen.*

349. **DESPUES DEL NIÑO ahogado, a tapar el pozo.** (After the child drowns, cover up the hole.) *Closing the barn door after the horse is stolen.*

350. **DESPUES DEL PISOTON—Usted dispense.** (After they step on you, they say, "Excuse me.") *Said after one does something stupid and begs the other person's pardon.*

351. **DESPUES DE OJO sacado no vale ¡Santa Lucia!** (After the eye is gone, "Heaven help me" is too late.) *What's done cannot be undone.*

352. **DESPUES DE UN BUEN SERVICIO, un mal pago.** (After good service, bad payment.) *Suggests not getting any appreciation for service done.*

353. **DE TAL BARBA, tal escama.** (From such a beard, such a scale.) *We should act according to our education and upbringing.*

354. **DE TAL JARRO, tal tepalcate.** (From such a jar, such a fragment.) *A chip off the old block.*

355. **DE TAL PALO, tal *estilla*.** (From such wood, such a chip.) *A chip off the old block.*

356. **DETRAS DE LA CRUZ está el diablo.** (Behind the cross lurks the devil.) *Advice to keep away from hypocrites.*

357. **DE TU CASA a la ajena, con la barriga llena.** (From your house to your neighbor's, go with a full stomach.) *Advises against taking advantage of a friend's kindness or confidence.*

358. **DE UNO EN UNO hasta que no quede ni uno.** (One by one until not one remain.) *One by one everything goes.*

359. **DIA de mucho, vísperas de nada.** (Day of plenty, eves of scarcity.) *Plenty today, want tomorrow.*

360. **DIA MARTES, ni te cases, ni te embarques.** (On Tuesday, neither marry nor go on a journey.) *In Spanish, Tuesday is unlucky like Friday the 13th in English.*

361. **DIA NUBLADO, mañanita larga.** (Cloudy day, long morning.) *Cloudy days bring boredom.*

362. **DIA NUBLOSO poco lluvioso.** (A cloudy day could bring a little rain.) *Great talkers are little doers.*

363. **DIAS de más, días de menos.** (Days of plenty, days of want.) *Scarcity follows plenty.*

364. **DIAS de unos, vísperas de otros.** (Days for some, eves for others.) *Life has its ups and downs.*

365. **DICEN que del agua fría nacen los tepocates.** (They say tadpoles are born from cold water.) *Said by a person as he tries to do the seemingly impossible.*

366. **DICHOS no rompen panzas pero adolecen corazones.** (Proverbs don't rip stomachs, but they do break hearts.) *Words do not kill but they do bring grief.*

367. **DIGOTELO, a ti, mi hija, y entiéndelo tú, mi nuera.** (I am telling you, my daughter, but it's meant for you, my daughter-in-law.) *Censures those who do not take a hint.*

368. **DILIGENCIA vale más que ciencia.** (Diligence is better than science.) *Resourcefulness over knowledge.*

369. **DIME con quién andas y te diré quién eres.** (Tell me whose company you keep and I'll tell you who you are.) *A man is known by the company he keeps.*

370. **DIME cuánto traes y te diré cuánto vales.** (Tell me how much money you have and I'll tell you how much you're worth.) *Money talks.*

371. **DINERO llama dinero.** (Money calls money.) *Money makes money.*

372. **DINEROS de sacristán: cantando vienen, cantando se van.** (The sexton's money: comes in singing, goes out singing.) *Like a gambler's money: easy come, easy go.*

373. **DINEROS son calidad.** (Money is quality.) *Money talks.*

374. **DIOS AMANECE para todos.** (God brings the dawn for everyone.) *Recommends that we enjoy our life and not be envious of others.*

375. **DIOS APRIETA pero no ahoga.** (God squeezes but does not choke us.) *All problems have some solution.*

376. **DIOS CASTIGA sin palo ni cuarta.** (God punishes without using a club or whip.) *God punishes man when he least expects it, and if he has it coming God's punishment is slow, but it does come.*

377. **DIOS da *almendras* al que no tiene muelas.** (God gives almonds to those who have no teeth.) *God brings good fortune to fools.*

378. **DIOS da el frío conforme a la ropa.** (God sends cold weather according to one's clothing.) *God tempers the wind to the shorn lamb.*

379. **DIOS da, pero no acarrea.** (God gives but He does not carry.) *God helps those who help themselves.*

380. **DIOS da y Dios quita.** (God gives and God takes.) *God gives and God takes away.*

381. **DIOS habla por el que calla.** (God speaks for him who keeps silent.) *God speaks for those who suffer in silence.*

382. **DIOS los cría y ellos se juntan.** (God raises them and they get together.) *Birds of a feather flock together.*

33

383. DIOS los hace y solitos se juntan. (God creates them and they get together.) *Birds of a feather flock together.*

384. DIOS manda el frío *asegún* la ropa. (God sends cold weather according to one's clothing.) *God tempers the wind to the shorn lamb.*

385. DIOS me libre del agua mansa (que de la brava me libro yo). (God save me from still water; I'll take care of the turbulent.) *Beware of still water.*

386. DIOS no castiga con palos ni azotes. (God does not punish with beatings or whippings.) *Punishment is lame, but it comes.*

387. DIOS no cumple antojas ni endereza jorobados. (God does not give in to whims nor does He straighten out hunchbacks.) *Said by a person when someone threatens him and he is not afraid of the threat.*

388. DIOS nos libre de un piojo resucitado. (God save us from a resurrected louse.) *God save us from a person who never had anything before; he becomes proud and arrogant.*

389. DIOS que da la llaga da la *medecina*. (God, Who gives the sore, gives the medicine.) *God, Who causes the wound, gives the cure.*

390. DIOS tarda pero no olvida. (God takes His time but He does not forget.) *God's will is slow but sure.*

391. DONDE BAILAN y tocan, todos se embocan. (Where they dance and play everyone goes in.) *Censures people who break into parties when they are not invited.*

392. DONDE ENTRA BEBER, sale saber. (Where drink goes in, knowledge goes out.) *When wine is in, wit is out.*

393. DONDE FUERZA VIENE, derecho se pierde. (Where force comes in, rights are lost.) *Might makes right.*

394. DONDE HABLAN LETRAS, callan barbas. (Where letters speak, beards keep silent.) *Documentary evidence is better than the assertions of the experienced.*

395. DONDE HAY AGUILILLAS, no la rifan gavilanes.

(Where there are eagles, hawks don't count.) *To the strong belong the spoils.*

396. DONDE HAY AMOR, hay dolor. (Where there's love, there's pain.) *Love makes one vulnerable to suffering.*

397. DONDE HAY AMOR no hay temor. (Where there's love there's no fear.) *Love has no fear.*

398. DONDE HAY GANA, hay maña. (Where there's a desire, there's a way.) *Where there's a will, there's a way.*

399. DONDE HAY HUMO, hay fuego. (Where there's smoke, there's fire.) *Where there's smoke, there's fire.*

400. DONDE HAY VOLUNTAD, hay modo. (Where there's a will, there's a way.) *Where there's a desire, there's a way.*

401. DONDE HAY YEGUAS, potros nacen. (Where there are mares, colts will be born.) *Where there's smoke, there's fire.*

402. DONDE LAS DAN, las toman. (Where they give, they receive.) *He who does wrong can expect to pay the consequences.*

403. DONDE LLORAN está el muerto. (Where there's mourning, there's a corpse.) *Where there's smoke, there's fire.*

404. DONDE LUMBRE ha habido, rescoldo queda. (Where there's been fire, embers remain.) *Where there's smoke, there's fire.*

405. DONDE MANDA CAPITAN no manda marinero. (Where there's a captain a sailor cannot command.) *To the strong belong the spoils.*

406. DONDE MENOS se piensa, salta la liebre. (Where you least expect it, the hare jumps.) *When we least expect it, good fortune comes our way.*

407. DONDE NO HAY HARINA, todo se vuelve remolina. (Where there's no flour, everything whirls.) *Financial straits bring discord.*

408. DONDE NO HAY REGLA, la necesidad la inventa. (Where there's no law, necessity invents one.) *Laws* *grow out of experience and necessity.*

409. DONDE QUIERA se cuecen habas. (Horse beans are boiled everywhere.) *We all make mistakes.*

410. DONDE TODO FALTA, Dios asiste. (Where everything else fails, God helps out.) *God does not turn away from the destitute.*

411. DONDE UNA PUERTA se cierra, *cien* se abren. (Where one door closes, a hundred open.) *Recommends not being dismayed in the face of adversity.*

412. ¡DONDE VAYA EL BUEY que no are! (Where can the ox go that he's not put to work!) *Wherever the needy go they have to work.*

413. DONDE VUELA GAVILAN, la paloma no aletea. (Where the falcon flies, the dove does not flit.) *To the strong belong the spoils.*

414. DOS *ABUJAS* no se pican. (Two needles cannot prick each other.) *Equal forces can't overpower each other.*

415. DOS *ALESNAS* no se pican. (Two awls cannot prick each other.) *Equal forces can't overpower each other.*

416. DOS GATOS en un costal no pueden estar. (Two cats cannot be contained in the same bag.) *Two people with similar defects cannot live together.*

417. DUELE MAS dedo que uña. (The finger hurts more than the fingernail.) *Blood is thicker than water.*

418. DUELE MAS el cuero que la camisa. (The skin hurts more than the shirt.) *Blood is thicker than water.*

419. DUELEN MAS los parches que las heridas. (The bandages hurt more than the wounds.) *Censures those who think more of their friends than their relatives.*

420. DURA LA MENTIRA mientras la verdad llega. (The lie lasts until the truth arrives.) *Lies have short lives.*

El pájaro que madruga se come el mejor gusano.
The early bird catches the worm.

421. **ECHANDO a perder se aprende.** (One learns by ruining things.) *One learns by trial and error.*

422. **EL AMIGO del rico es un peso en la *bolsa*.** (The friend of the rich man is a dollar in his pocket.) *With the rich, money talks.*

423. **EL AMIGO que no da y el cuchillo que no corta, que se pierdan, poco importa.** (The friend that doesn't give and the knife that doesn't cut, if lost, matters little.) *The friend that does not share his things and the knife that does not cut, may as well be lost, for they are worthless.*

424. **EL AMIGO viejo, el mejor espejo.** (An old friend, a better reflection.) *Our best mirror is an old friend.*

425. **EL AMOR de lejos es pa los pendejos.** (Love from afar is for fools.) *Love at a distance is for fools.*

426. **EL AMOR no lo parieron los burros.** (Love was not begat by donkeys.) *Love is no fool.*

427. **EL AMOR que ha sido brasa, de repente vuelve a arder.** (Love that has been a cinder can easily reignite.) *Where there's smoke, there's fire.*

428. **EL AMOR y el melón no pueden ser ocultos.** (Love and

a cantaloupe cannot be hidden.) *It's hard to hide one's love for someone.*

429. **EL ARBOL se conoce por su fruto.** (The tree is known by its fruit.) *A man is known by his works.*

430. **EL BARRIGON ni aunque lo fajen.** (A fat person will be fat even if he's bound.) *You can't change a man's character.*

431. **EL BIEN, cuando más querido, más pronto se ve perdido.** (When we're closer to something dear to us we seem to lose it.) *Comments on the transitoriness of life.*

432. **EL BIEN no es conocido hasta que es perdido.** (Good fortune is never appreciated until it is lost.) *We never miss the sunshine until the shadows come.*

433. **EL BIEN y el mal a la cara sal.** (Good and evil show up to one's face.) *It is hard to hide one's emotions.*

434. **EL BUEN PADRE en su casa comienza.** (The good parent begins at home.) *Charity begins at home.*

435. **EL *CABRESTO* se troza por lo más delgado.** (The rope breaks where it's thinnest.) *A chain is as strong as its weakest link.*

436. **EL CAMARON que se duerme se lo lleva la corriente.** (The shrimp that falls asleep is carried away by the current.) *Don't let the grass grow under your feet.*

437. **EL CAMBIO de pasto engorda la ternera.** (A change of pasture fattens the calf.) *Variety is the spice of life.*

438. **EL CARBON que ha sido brasa con poquita lumbre tiene.** (A coal that was live once needs little fire.) *It's easy to lapse back into a bad habit.*

439. **EL CHISME agrada, el chismoso enfada.** (Gossip pleases, but the gossiper annoys.) *An expression of dislike for gossipers.*

440. **EL CHISTE no es mear, sino que el chorro haga espuma.** (The trick is not to piss, but to get the spurt to foam.) *Thinking you can do a job and being able to do it are two different things.*

441. **EL CHISTE no es ser hermosa, sino saber presumir.**

(The trick is not to be beautiful but to know how to be charming.) *In addition to her beauty, a girl has to be charming in order to be successful.*

442. **EL COMAL le dijo a la olla,—¡Qué cola tan prieta tienes!** (The griddle said to the pot, "What a black tail you have!") *The pot calling the kettle black.*

443. **EL COMAL le dijo a la olla,—¡Qué tiznada estás!** (The griddle said to the pot, "How black you look!") *The pot calling the kettle black.*

444. **EL CONSEJO de la mujer es poco y el que no lo escucha es loco.** (A woman's advice is infrequent, and he who does not listen to it is crazy.) *Recommends taking women's advice.*

445. **EL DAR Y TENER, seso ha menester.** (Giving and keeping need brains.) *It takes thought to give and to hold on to your possessions.*

446. **EL DERECHO nace del hecho.** (Right is born from the deed.) *A person is entitled to his right only if he has done something to deserve it.*

447. **EL DESEO embellece lo feo.** (Desire beautifies what is ugly.) *Beauty is in the eye of the beholder.*

448. **EL DIABLO, harto de carne, se metió fraile.** (The devil, fed up on meat, became a friar.) *Young sinner, old saint.*

449. **EL DIABLO lo que sabe es por viejo y no por diablo.** (The devil knows what he knows because he is old and not because he is the devil.) *Experience is the best teacher.*

450. **EL DIA que te casas, o te curas o te matas.** (The day you marry you either get cured or killed.) *Marriage settles a person.*

451. **EL DIENTE miente, la cana engaña y la arruga me deja duda.** (The tooth lies, gray hairs deceive, and wrinkles leave me in doubt.) *Appearances are deceiving.*

452. **EL DINERO llama al dinero.** (Money calls money.) *Money makes money.*

453. **EL DINERO no es santo pero hace milagros.** (Money is

no saint but it does perform miracles.) *Money talks.*

454. **EL DINERO se paga pero el favor no.** (Money is paid back but not the favor.) *The moral value of a favor is far more important than money.*

455. **EL DINERO todo lo puede.** (Money can do everything.) *Money talks.*

456. **EL EJERCICIO hace al maestro.** (Practice makes the teacher.) *Practice makes perfect.*

457. **EL ESTREÑIDO muere de *cursios*.** (The constipated person dies of diarrhea.) *A greedy person can lose everything he has and become destitute.*

458. **EL FAVOR recibido debe ser correspondido.** (A favor received must be returned.) *Chides those who forget to repay favors done to them.*

459. **EL FLOJO y el mezquino andan dos veces el camino.** (The lazy and the miser go twice over the same road.) *The lazy and the reluctant have to do a task over again.*

460. **EL FRAILE que pide pan, carne come si se la dan.** (The monk that asks for bread will take meat if they offer it to him.) *Some people will take a mile if you give them an inch.*

461. **EL GATO escaldado del agua fría huye.** (The scalded cat runs from cold water.) *Once burnt, twice shy.*

462. **EL GOLPE del sartén aunque no duele tizna.** (Even if a blow with a frying pan does not hurt, it still blackens one.) *Slander, although known as such, leaves a stain on one's reputation.*

463. **EL HABITO no hace al monje.** (Clothes do not make the monk.) *Appearances are deceiving.*

464. **EL HABLAR es más fácil que el probar.** (Talking about a thing is easier than proving it.) *Talk is cheap.*

465. **EL HAMBRE es lo bueno, no la comida.** (Hunger is the thing, not the food.) *Hunger is the best sauce.*

466. **EL HAMBRE las tumba y la vanidad las levanta.** (Hunger knocks them down and vanity raises them.) *Cen-*

40

sures those persons in economic straits who pretend not to be badly off financially.

467. **EL HIJO bueno alegra al padre.** (A good son is his father's pride.) *A good son is a joy to his father.*

468. **EL HIJO del asno dos veces rebuzna al día.** (The son of the ass brays twice a day.) *Like father, like son.*

469. **EL HILO se revienta por lo más delgado.** (Thread breaks where it's thinnest.) *A chain is as strong as its weakest link.*

470. **EL HOMBRE, como el oso, entre más feo, más hermoso.** (Man, like a bear, the uglier he is, the handsomer he looks.) *Preference for a caveman type of companion.*

471. **EL HOMBRE en su casa es rey.** (Man in his own home is king.) *A man's home is his castle.*

472. **EL HOMBRE es fuego, la mujer estopa, llega el diablo y sopla.** (Man is fire, woman's tow; comes the devil, the coals blow.) *It doesn't take much for a man and a woman to get close to each other.*

473. **EL HOMBRE hace y Dios deshace.** (Man proposes, God disposes.) *God always has the last word in determining man's fate.*

474. **EL HOMBRE propone y Dios dispone.** (Man proposes, God disposes.) *God always has the last word in determining man's fate.*

475. **EL INFIERNO está empedrado de buenas intenciones.** (Hell is paved with good intentions.) *Censures those people who, despite all intentions, set out to do a thing and never do it.*

476. **EL INTERES tiene pies.** (Interest has feet.) *People do things in a hurry when they're for their own benefit.*

477. **EL LOBO pierde los dientes pero no las mientes.** (The wolf loses his teeth but not his ways.) *The leopard can't change his spots.*

478. **EL LUNES ni las gallinas ponen.** (On Mondays not even chickens lay.) *Monday is a rough day.*

41

479. **EL MAESTRO ciruela enseña sin haber tenido escuela.** (Master Pool has taken up teaching without ever having had any school.) *Censures those people who think teaching needs no preparation.*

480. **EL MAL ESCRIBANO le echa la culpa a la pluma.** (The bad writer lays the blame on his pen.) *Chides people who always look for excuses for their failures.*

481. **EL MARTES, ni te cases ni te embarques.** (Marry not nor go on a journey on a Tuesday.) *In Spanish, Tuesday is unlucky like Friday the 13th in English.*

482. **EL MAS AMIGO es traidor y el más verdadero miente.** (Your closest friend will betray you and the most truthful will lie.) *Be careful whom you trust.*

483. **EL MEJOR NADADOR perece en el agua.** (The best swimmer perishes in the water.) *We all make mistakes.*

484. **EL MELON y el casamiento ha de ser de acercamiento.** (Cantaloupes and marriage must be chosen with great care.) *Recommends exercising great care in choosing one's future spouse.*

485. **EL MIEDO no anda en burro.** (Fear does not travel on a donkey.) *Fear makes a man run fast.*

486. **EL MUCHO HABLAR descompone.** (Too much talk spoils everything.) *Too much talk distorts things.*

487. **EL MUERTO a la sepultura y el vivo a la travesura.** (The dead to the grave and the survivor to his pranks.) *Censures a short period of mourning.*

488. **EL MUERTO al hoyo y el vivo al bollo.** (The dead to the grave and the survivor to the feast.) *Censures a short period of mourning.*

489. **EL MUERTO al pozo y el vivo al negocio.** (The dead to the grave and the survivor to his business.) *Censures a short period of mourning.*

490. **EL MUERTO al pozo y el vivo al retozo.** (The dead to the grave and the survivor to his play.) *Censures a short period of mourning.*

42

491. EL MUERTO y el arrimado a los tres días apestan. (The corpse and the unwelcome guest begin to smell after three days.) *Censures people who take advantage of visits to friends.*

492. EL OJO del amo engorda el caballo. (The eye of the master fattens the horse.) *Under the supervision of the owner, the estate prospers.*

493. EL PAJARO que madruga se come el mejor gusano. (The early bird eats the best worm.) *The early bird catches the worm.*

494. EL PAN ajeno hace al hijo bueno. (Someone else's bread makes one's son good.) *One's children behave better under a stranger's supervision.*

495. EL PAN comido y la compañía deshecha. (The bread eaten, the company dispersed.) *Criticizes those people who desert their friends once they cannot expect further favors from them.*

496. EL PAN partido Dios lo aumenta. (God blesses the bread that is shared.) *Bread that is shared goes far.*

497. EL PEDIR no destruye, el dar es lo que empobrece. (Asking hurts no one; it's the giving that impoverishes.) *Advises against being too liberal in giving what one has.*

498. EL PEOR de los males es tratar con animales. (The worst of evils is to deal with beasts.) *A commentary on having to put up with uncouth people.*

499. EL PEOR sordo es el que no quiere oír. (None so deaf as those who will not listen.) *Censures those who pretend not to be listening because it is not to their advantage.*

500. EL PEREZOSO y el mezquino andan dos veces el camino. (The lazy and the miser walk twice over the same road.) *The lazy do things reluctantly and twice to get them done right; the miser does not take enough money to market and has to return home for more.*

501. EL PERRO le manda al gato y el gato a su cola. (The dog orders the cat and the cat orders its tail.) *Passing the buck.*

502. **EL PERRO que come caca, si no la come la huele.** (The dog that eats excrement, smells it if he doesn't eat it.) *Comment on how hard it is to get rid of a bad habit.*

503. **EL PESCADO por la boca muere.** (Fish meet death through their mouths.) *People often talk too much, and tactlessly.*

504. **EL PESCADO y el arrimado a los tres días apestan.** (Fish and the unwelcome guest smell after three days.) *Advises against overstaying one's welcome.*

505. **EL PEZ que busca anzuelo, busca su duelo.** (The fish that goes for the hook looks for his funeral.) *If you look for trouble, you find it.*

506. **EL POCO HABLAR es oro, el mucho hablar es lodo.** (Talking moderately is gold, talking excessively is mud.) *Silence is golden.*

507. **EL PROMETER no empobrece, el dar es lo que aniquila.** (Promising does not impoverish; it's giving that destroys.) *Advises against being overly liberal in giving what one has.*

508. **EL QUE A BUEN ARBOL se arrima, buena sombra lo cobija.** (He who sits near a large tree will find good shade.) *He who has powerful backers attains great advantage.*

509. **EL QUE ADELANTE no mira, atrás se queda.** (He who does not look ahead remains behind.) *Foresight over hindsight.*

510. **EL QUE A DIOS busca, a Dios halla.** (He who looks for God, finds Him.) *Seek and ye shall find.*

511. **EL QUE A DOS AMOS sirve, con uno queda mal.** (He who serves two masters neglects one of them.) *You can't serve two masters.*

512. **EL QUE A FEA ama, hermosa le parece.** (He who loves an ugly woman thinks her beautiful.) *Beauty is in the eye of the beholder.*

513. **EL QUE A HIERRO mata, a hierro muere.** (He who kills with a weapon, is killed by a weapon.) *He who kills by*

the sword, dies by the sword.

514. **EL QUE AL ALBA SE LEVANTA, tiene su salud y en su trabajo adelanta.** (He who rises early enjoys good health and gets ahead in his work.) *Early to bed and early to rise makes a man healthy, wealthy, and wise.*

515. **EL QUE AL CIELO escupe, en la cara le cae.** (He who spits upward gets the spittle in his face.) *People that live in glass houses shouldn't throw stones.*

516. **EL QUE ANDA entre la mierda, algo se le pega.** (He who walks in excretion is sure to be smeared.) *Advises us to avoid companions who cannot contribute much to our personal improvement but can harm us instead.*

517. **EL QUE ANDA entre los lobos, a aullar se enseña.** (He who keeps company with wolves will learn to howl.) *A man is known by the company he keeps.*

518. **EL QUE SOLO se ríe, de sus maldades se acuerda.** (He who laughs to himself is remembering an old prank.) *He who laughs to himself is reminded of some old prank.*

519. **EL QUE A TODOS quiere saludar, pronto rompe su sombrero.** (He who wants to greet everyone soon tears his hat.) *One can't please everybody.*

520. **EL QUE A TU CASA no va, en su casa no te quiere.** (He who does not go to your house does not want you in his.) *Reproaches those who ask us to visit them when they never visit us.*

521. **EL QUE BOCA TIENE, a Roma va.** (He who has a tongue gets to Rome.) *Recommends that one not be shy in asking one's way.*

522. **El QUE CALLA, otorga.** (He who keeps silent consents.) *Silence gives consent.*

523. **EL QUE CANTA, sus males espanta.** (He who sings is frightening away his woes.) *People often hum or sing to pretend they are not worried.*

524. **EL QUE COME Y CANTA, loco se levanta.** (He who eats and sings at the same time goes crazy.) *Said to children who sing at the table while eating.*

45

525. **EL QUE CON LECHE se quema hasta al jocoque le sopla.** (He who gets burnt with milk tries to cool the buttermilk.) *Once burnt, twice shy.*

526. **EL QUE CON LOBOS anda, a aullar se enseña.** (He who keeps company with wolves learns to howl.) *Bad habits are acquired from bad companions.*

527. **EL QUE CON NIÑOS se acuesta amanece mojado.** (He who sleeps with children awakens wet.) *Recommends against relying on children's opinions.*

528. **EL QUE CORRE, largar quiere.** (He who runs fast wants to leave you behind.) *Said of those who improve themselves and then try to do better than others.*

529. **EL QUE DA lo que tiene, a pedir pronto viene.** (He who gives what he has soon comes begging.) *Recommends against giving away one's possessions.*

530. **EL QUE DA lo que tiene, el diablo se ríe de él.** (He who gives away what he has is laughed at by the devil.) *Recommends against being too liberal with one's things.*

531. **EL QUE DA PAN a perro ajeno, pierde el pan y pierde el perro.** (He who gives bread to a stray dog loses the bread and the dog.) *Strangers normally do not appreciate things people do for them.*

532. **EL QUE DA PRIMERO, da dos veces.** (He who strikes first, strikes twice.) *Praises those who get ahead in some task.*

533. **EL QUE DA RAZON del camino es porque lo tiene andado.** (He who gives you information about the road does so because he has travelled it.) *People usually speak from experience.*

534. **EL QUE DA Y QUITA, con el diablo se desquita.** (He who gives then retrieves a gift will answer to the devil.) *Censures someone who gives something and then wants it back.*

535. **EL QUE DE AFUERA VIENE, de tu casa te echará.** (He who comes from afar will put you out of your house.) *A comment on how a person will often be pushed out*

46

by a stranger in matters of love, position, or even employment.

536. EL QUE DE AJENO SE VISTE, en la calle lo desnudan. (He who dresses in someone else's clothes can be left naked on the street.) *Censures people who attribute undeserved merit to themselves.*

537. EL QUE DEJA para otro día, de Dios desconfía. (He who saves things till tomorrow has no trust in God.) *Said by people who want to eat everything now.*

538. EL QUE DE MAÑANA se levanta, con cualquier bulto se espanta. (The early riser is easily frightened.) *Said by persons who refuse to get up early.*

539. EL QUE DE MAÑANA se levanta, en su trabajo adelanta. (He who rises early gets ahead in his work.) *Praises the early riser.*

540. EL QUE DESDE CHICO es guaje, hasta acocote no para. (He who is a fool in his childhood will not go beyond being an acocote.) *Stupidity grows with age.*

541. EL QUE DESEA MAL a su vecino, el suyo viene en camino. (He who wishes his neighbor some ill, beckons his own.) *Recommends that we use the Golden Rule.*

542. EL QUE DE SU CASA se aleja, no la halla como la deja. (He who leaves home never finds it as he left it.) *People who leave their home should expect changes on their return and should not complain.*

543. EL QUE DUERME en casa ajena, de mañana se levanta. (He who sleeps in another's house rises early.) *He who sleeps in another's house is the first one to get up.*

544. EL QUE ENVIUDA y se casa, de loco se pasa. (A widower who remarries is more than crazy.) *A widower who remarries is twice a fool.*

545. EL QUE ES BARRIGON, aunque lo faje un arriero. (He who is fat will be fat even though a muleteer may gird him.) *It is difficult to change a person's character.*

546. EL QUE ES BUEN GALLO, en cualquier gallinero canta. (A good rooster will crow in any chicken coop.) *Praises a man who is unafraid.*

47

547. **EL QUE ES BUEN JUEZ, por su casa comienza.** (The good judge begins at home.) *Practice what you preach.*

548. **EL QUE ES BUEN PATO, en el aire nada.** (The good duck swims in the air.) *Suggests that the smart have no problem doing what they want to do.*

549. **EL QUE ES CORTO no entra al cielo y el que es largo se atraviesa.** (The timid don't get to heaven and the aggressive block their own way.) *Recommends striking a happy medium in any undertaking.*

550. **EL QUE ESCUCHA, mierda embucha.** (He who eavesdrops eats excrement.) *He who eavesdrops might get his feelings hurt by what he hears.*

551. **EL QUE ESPERA, desespera (y muere desesperado).** (He who waits despairs [and dies of despair].) *He who lives in hope dies of despair.*

552. **EL QUE ES SANTO y resbala, hasta el infierno no para.** (He who is saintly and slips up doesn't stop until he gets to hell.) *A good person who errs goes to the dogs.*

553. **EL QUE ESTA HECHO al mal, el bien le ofende.** (He who is used to discomfort will be offended if offered comfort.) *Not everybody appreciates others' luxuries.*

554. **EL QUE ESTA MATADO, se pandea.** (He who has a sore will flinch.) *He who bears a stigma feels hurt if someone points it out.*

555. **EL QUE ES TONTO, toca 'l acordeón, come mucho pan y escribe buena letra.** (He who is stupid plays the accordion, eats a lot of bread, and has a good handwriting.) *Some people think they know everything.*

556. **EL QUE EVITA la tentación, evita el pecado.** (He who avoids the temptation avoids the sin.) *Avoid temptation.*

557. **EL QUE FIA, salió a cobrar.** (The man who sells on credit goes out to collect.) *A curt way of saying the store does not sell on credit.*

558. **EL QUE GUARDA para otro día, de Dios desconfía.** (He who saves for another day does not trust in God.) *Said by people who don't want to save.*

48

559. EL QUE HABLA del camino es porque lo tiene andado. (He who talks of the road does so because he knows it.) *Some people censure others for faults they have committed themselves.*

560. EL QUE HABLA mucho pronto calla. (He who talks a lot soon becomes silent.) *He who talks too much runs out of things to say.*

561. EL QUE HA de ser barrigón, aunque lo fajen. (He who was born to be fat will be fat even though they may gird him.) *It's hard to change one's character.*

562. EL QUE HA DE SER medio, aunque ande entre los tostones. (He who is destined to be a dime will remain so even though he is surrounded by fifty-cent pieces.) *It's hard to rise above a low economic condition.*

563. EL QUE HA de ser pobre, más que ande entre el dinero. (He who is destined to be poor will remain so even though he is surrounded by money.) *Poverty was not meant to prosper.*

564. EL QUE HA DE SER REAL sencillo, aunque ande entre los doblones. (He who is destined to be a simple coin will remain so even though he is surrounded by gold coins.) *The common person is common even among the elite.*

565. EL QUE HAMBRE TIENE, en tortillas piensa. (He who is hungry thinks of tortillas.) *A desire can become an obsession.*

566. EL QUE HUYE del costo huye del provecho. (He who avoids cost does not benefit.) *Cheap things turn out to be expensive.*

567. EL QUE HUYE VA a su casa y cuenta lo que pasa. (He who runs away is able to get home and tell what happened.) *He that fights and runs away may live to fight another day.*

568. EL QUE LA HACE, la paga. (He who harms someone pays for it.) *As you sow, so shall you reap.*

569. EL QUE LARGA VIDA vive, mucho mal ha de pasar.

(He who lives a long life, suffers much.) *A comment on old age being a series of ills.*

570. **EL QUE LE BUSCA tres pies al gato, le halla cuatro.** (He who looks for three paws on a cat discovers that it has four.) *A person who looks for trouble has no trouble finding it.*

571. **EL QUE LE LAVA la cara al burro pierde su tiempo y pierde el jabón.** (He who washes a donkey's face loses his time and his soap.) *Not everybody appreciates favors done for them.*

572. **EL QUE LENGUA tiene, a Roma va.** (He who has a tongue gets to Rome.) *Advice against being overly shy.*

573. **EL QUE LLEGA primero, muele primero.** (He who arrives first, grinds first.) *First come, first served.*

574. **EL QUE LUCE entre las ollas no luce entre las señoras.** (He who shines among the pots and pans makes an impression on the ladies.) *Recommends good education and training to get ahead in life.*

575. **EL QUE MADRUGA, come pechuga.** (He who gets up early eats chicken breast.) *First come, first served.*

576. **EL QUE MAL anda, bien no espere.** (He who leads an evil life can expect no good.) *As you sow, so shall you reap.*

577. **EL QUE MALAS mañas ha, tarde o nunca las perderá.** (He who has bad habits will lose them late in life or never.) *Bad habits are difficult to uproot.*

578. **EL QUE MAL CANTA, bien le suena.** (He who sings badly thinks he sings well.) *We are all blind to our own defects.*

579. **EL QUE MAL HACE, bien no espere.** (He who does evil cannot expect anything good.) *He who kills by the sword dies by the sword.*

580. **EL QUE MAL PIENSA, mal hace.** (He who thinks evil, does evil.) *Evil thoughts, evil deeds.*

581. **EL QUE MAL VIVE, el miedo le sigue.** (He who does

evil is followed by fear.) *Conscience does make cowards of us all.*

582. EL QUE MAS ALTO sube, más grande porrazo se da. (He who climbs higher receives the heaviest blow.) *The higher they climb, the harder they fall.*

583. EL QUE MAS CORRE, menos vuela. (He who runs fastest flies slower.) *Two swift arrives as tardy as too slow.*

584. EL QUE MAS MIRA, menos ve. (He who sees more, sees less.) *Excessive discernment is harmful.*

585. EL QUE MENOS CORRE, vuela. (He who runs less is flying.) *A reference to those who are observant of their surroundings while pretending indifference.*

586. EL QUE METE PAZ, saca más. (He who brings peace gets more than peace.) *Censures meddlers.*

587. EL QUE MUCHO ABARCA, poco aprieta. (He who grasps tightly holds nothing fast.) *Don't bite off more than you can chew.*

588. EL QUE MUCHO CORRE, pronto para. (He who runs much soon stops.) *He who starts a task full of enthusiasm soon gives up.*

589. EL QUE MUCHO DUERME, poco aprende. (He that sleeps much learns little.) *Don't let the grass grow under your feet.*

590. EL QUE MUCHO HABLA, mucho yerra. (He that speaks much errs much.) *Big talkers, big mistakes.*

591. EL QUE MUCHO HABLA, pronto se calla. (He who talks much soon keeps silent.) *A fool, when he hath spoken, hath done all.*

592. EL QUE MUCHO HUELE es porque mucho jiede. (He who goes around smelling everything does so because he himself smells.) *Reproaches those people who continuously criticize defects in others and who may be victims of those same defects.*

593. EL QUE MUCHO REZA, presto acaba. (He who prays a lot soon finishes.) *A fool's bolt is soon shot.*

594. EL QUE MUCHO SE DESPIDE, pocas ganas tiene de irse. (He who keeps saying goodbye doesn't feel like leaving.) *Parting is such sweet sorrow.*

595. EL QUE NACE pa la yunta, del cielo le caen los cuernos. (He who is destined for the yoke gets his horns from heaven.) *He who puts up with being a cuckold deserves no pity.*

596. EL QUE NACE pa maceta, no pasa del corredor. (He who is born to be a flowerpot won't go beyond the hall.) *He who is dull as a child will be stupid as a man.*

597. EL QUE NACE PARA POBRE, mientras viva lo ha de ser. (He who is born poor will remain poor as long as he lives.) *Acceptance of poverty.*

598. EL QUE NACE PARA TRISTE, aunque le canten canciones. (He who is born to be sad will be sad even though they sing him songs.) *It is hard to change someone's disposition.*

599. EL QUE NACIO pa panzón, aunque lo fajen de niño. (He who was born to be fat will remain so even though he may be tightly bound as a child.) *What is bred in the bone will never come out of the flesh.*

600. EL QUE NACIO PARA BUEY, del cielo le caen los cuernos. (He who was born to be an ox gets his horns from heaven.) *Some men are predestined to become cuckolds.*

601. EL QUE NACIO PARA BUEY, desde la cuna da topes. (He who was born to be an ox starts butting in the cradle.) *What is bred in the bone will never come out of the flesh.*

602. EL QUE NACIO PA TAMAL del cielo le caen las hojas. (He who was born to be a tamale gets his husks from heaven.) *He who was born to be slow will be slow.*

603. EL QUE NADA arriesga, nada tiene. (He who risks nothing has nothing.) *Nothing ventured, nothing gained.*

604. EL QUE NADA no se ahoga. (He who swims does not drown.) *Sink or swim.*

605. EL QUE NADA TIENE, nada le quitan. (One can't take anything from one who has nothing.) *A warning to beware of people who have nothing to lose.*

606. EL QUE NADA TIENE, nada pierde. (He who has nothing has nothing to lose.) *A warning to beware of people who have nothing to lose.*

607. EL QUE NO ARRIESGA, no gana. (He who doesn't risk doesn't win.) *Nothing ventured, nothing gained.*

608. EL QUE NO COJEA, renquea. (He who doesn't limp is lame.) *No one is perfect.*

609. EL QUE NO DA de enamorado menos da de casado. (He who gives nothing when he's courting will give less when he's married.) *A miser is always a miser.*

610. EL QUE NO HABLA, Dios no lo oye. (He who doesn't speak up is not heard by God.) *Faint heart never won fair lady.*

611. EL QUE NO LLORA, no mama. (The baby who does not cry does not get milk.) *The wheel that squeaks gets the most grease.*

612. EL QUE NO MIRA adelante, atrás se queda. (He who does not look ahead remains behind.) *Advises us to use foresight.*

613. EL QUE NO OYE consejo, no llega a viejo. (He who doesn't listen to advice doesn't get to be old.) *Suggests that listening to the voice of the experienced may benefit us greatly.*

614. EL QUE NO PERDONA a su enemigo no tiene a Dios por amigo. (He who doesn't forgive his enemy doesn't have God for a friend.) *To err is human, to forgive, divine.*

615. EL QUE NO SE ARRIESGA no pasa la mar. (He who doesn't take a risk doesn't cross the sea.) *Nothing ventured, nothing gained.*

616. EL QUE NO SE MUERE, se vuelve a ver. (He who doesn't die is seen again.) *It's a small world.*

617. EL QUE NUNCA ha tenido y llega a tener, loco se quiere volver. (He who has never had anything and suddenly acquires things almost goes crazy.) *A comment on people's reaction when they suddenly acquire material possessions.*

618. EL QUE PAGA lo que debe, sabe lo que tiene. (He who pays what he owes knows what he has.) *He who pays his debts increases his wealth.*

619. EL QUE PARA guaje nace, hasta jícara no para. (He who is born to be a gourd will only get to be a dipper.) *Everyone acts within his own mental capacity.*

620. EL QUE PARTE y comparte guarda para sí la mejor parte. (He who divides and shares keeps the best part for himself.) *The person who divides things among several people usually is selfish enough to keep the best for himself.*

621. EL QUE PERDONA a su enemigo, a Dios tiene por amigo. (He who forgives his enemy wins God for a friend.) *To err is human, to forgive, divine.*

622. EL QUE PERSEVERA alcanza. (He who perseveres goes far.) *He who perseveres reaches his goal.*

623. EL QUE PORFIA, mata venado. (He who pursues kills his deer.) *He who perseveres goes far.*

624. EL QUE POR OTRO pide, por sí aboga. (He who wishes ill for another may bring it on himself.) *He who wishes misfortune on another might get it himself.*

625. EL QUE POR su gusto es buey, hasta la coyunda lambe. (He who chooses to be an ox will even lick the strap.) *Don't complain of being mistreated if you enjoy it.*

626. EL QUE POR su gusto muere, hasta la muerte le sabe. (He who dies willingly savors death.) *Don't complain of being mistreated if you enjoy it.*

627. EL QUE PRESTA lo que ha menester, el diablo se ríe de él. (He who lends what he needs gets laughed at by the devil.) *Criticizes the lack of judgment of people who lend the very things they need.*

54

628. **EL QUE PRIMERO llega al molino muele primero.** (The one who gets first to the mill is the one that grinds first.) *First come, first served.*

629. **EL QUE QUIERA tener fortuna y fama, no le pegue el sol en la cama.** (He who wants fame and fortune must not let the sun find him in bed.) *It takes hard work to attain fame and fortune.*

630. **EL QUE QUIERE AZUL celeste, que le cueste.** (He who wants azure blue should pay for it.) *Personal whims must be paid for.*

631. **EL QUE QUIERE BAILE, que pague músico.** (He who wants the dance should hire a musician.) *Special things cost a little extra.*

632. **EL QUE QUIERE LA COL, quiere las hojas de alrededor.** (He who likes the cabbage likes the leaves around it.) *Love me, love my dog.*

633. **EL QUE QUIERE LA GLORIA tiene que rezar.** (He who wants a place in heaven has to pray.) *If you want material things you have to work for them.*

634. **EL QUE QUIERE LLEGAR a viejo, debe comenzar temprano.** (He who wants to become old must start early.) *Those who would be young when they are old must be old when they are young.*

635. **EL QUE QUIERE, puede.** (He who wants to, can.) *Where there's a will, there's a way.*

636. **EL QUE REGALA, bien vende si el que lo recibe lo entiende.** (He who gives a gift is a good salesman if the recipient understands.) *Gifts are good investments.*

637. **EL QUE REPARTE y comparte**
y al repartir tiene tino
siempre deja de *contino*
para sí la mejor parte.
(He that divides and distributes
And has a knack at dividing
Always leaves the best part for himself.)
The person who distributes things generally keeps the best for himself.

55

638. EL QUE RIE al último ríe mejor. (He who laughs at the end laughs best.) *He who laughs last laughs best.*

639. EL QUE SALE a bailar, pierde su lugar. (He who gets up to dance loses his seat.) *A person who gives up his position should not complain if another replaces him.*

640. EL QUE SE ACUESTA con niños ya sabe cómo amanece. (He who goes to sleep with children well knows how he'll be when he wakes up.) *Advice against relying on the opinion of children.*

641. EL QUE SE CASA, por todo pasa. (He who gets married endures everything.) *Marriage brings a lot of hardships with it.*

642. EL QUE SE FUE pa la villa perdió su silla. (He who left for the village has lost his seat.) *A person who gives up his place should not complain if someone else replaces him.*

643. EL QUE SE HACE miel se lo comen las moscas. (He who turns into honey is swarmed by flies.) *People take advantage of those persons who are overly nice.*

644. EL QUE SE HA quemado con leche, hasta al jocoque le sopla. (He who has burned himself with hot milk will blow on his buttermilk.) *Once burnt, twice shy.*

645. EL QUE SE METE a redentor sale crucificado. (He who becomes a redeemer emerges crucified.) *Advises against sticking out one's neck for the ungrateful.*

646. EL QUE SE MUERE por otro, ni el campo santo merece. (He who dies for another doesn't deserve the plot where he's buried.) *Chides foolish persons who say they would give their life for another.*

647. EL QUE SE PARA a bailar pierde su lugar. (He who gets up to dance loses his place.) *A person who gives up his place should not complain if someone else replaces him.*

648. EL QUE SE RASCA, sarna tiene. (He who scratches himself has an itch.) *Excusing oneself usually indicates one is to blame.*

649. EL QUE SE RIE al último se ríe más bonito. (He who laughs last laughs the most merrily.) *He who laughs last laughs best.*

650. EL QUE SE VA pa la villa, pierde su silla. (He who goes to the village loses his seat.) *A person who gives up his place should not complain if someone else replaces him.*

651. EL QUE SE VE prevenido no se ve abatido. (He who is prepared is not defeated.) *Forewarned is forearmed.*

652. EL QUE SIEMBRA cadillos recoge espinas. (He who sows burrs will reap thorns.) *As you sow, so shall you reap.*

653. EL QUE SIEMBRA EN TIERRA ajena, hasta la semilla pierde. (He who sows in someone else's land loses even the seed.) *Not everyone appreciates the things we do for them.*

654. EL QUE SOLO se come su gallo, solo encierra su caballo. (He who eats his rooster by himself puts his horse in the barn by himself.) *People are not likely to help a person who doesn't help others.*

655. EL QUE SOLO SE RIE, de sus maldades se acuerda. (He who laughs to himself must be remembering an old prank.) *He who laughs to himself is remembering an amusing incident.*

656. EL QUE TE alaba y lisonjea, su bien y tu mal desea. (He who praises and plays up to you wants to improve his position and cause your ruin.) *Advises against trusting flatterers.*

657. EL QUE TE DA un hueso no quiere verte morir. (He who gives you a bone doesn't want to see you die.) *Recommends trusting people who help us.*

658. EL QUE TE IDOLATRA más, confía más en su daño. (Beware of the person who idolizes you most.) *Beware of Greeks bearing gifts.*

659. EL QUE TEMPRANO se levanta con cualquier bulto se espanta. (He who arises early will become frightened easily.) *Said by people who don't want to get up early.*

660. **EL QUE TEMPRANO SE MOJA tiene tiempo de secarse.** (He who gets drenched early has time to dry.) *An early morning drink will give us time to sober up. A bad experience early in life gives us ample time to learn a good lesson.*

661. **EL QUE TE QUIERE te hace llorar.** (He who loves you will make you cry.) *Spare the rod and spoil the child.*

662. **EL QUE TERQUEA mata venado.** (He who perseveres kills his deer.) *Slow and steady wins the race.*

663. **EL QUE TIENE BOCA, se equivoca.** (He who has a mouth will make a mistake.) *We all make mistakes.*

664. **EL QUE TIENE CUATRO y gasta cinco no necesita bolsa.** (He who has four and spends five does not need a purse.) *A warning against spendthrifts.*

665. **EL QUE TIENE HIJO varón, no dé voces al ladrón.** (Let he who has a son not shout at the thief.) *Let no one speak ill of others lest the same misfortune happen to him.*

666. **EL QUE TIENE MAS saliva traga más pinole.** (He who has more saliva swallows more corn powder.) *The smarter the person, the more advantages he has.*

667. **EL QUE TIENE TEJADO de vidrio que no tire piedras al de su vecino.** (The man who has a glass roof must not cast stones at his neighbor's.) *People who live in glass houses shouldn't throw stones.*

668. **EL QUE TIENE TIENDA, que la atienda, si no, que la venda.** (Let he who has a store mind it; otherwise, he should sell it.) *Everyone should look after and protect his property.*

669. **EL QUE TODO lo quiere, todo lo pierde.** (He who wants it all, loses it all.) *All covet, all lose.*

670. **EL QUE TONTO va a la guerra, tonto viene de ella.** (He who is a fool when he goes to war is still a fool when he returns.) *Travelling benefits only the intelligent.*

671. **EL RICO, como el marrano, no rinde hasta que muere.** (The rich man, like a pig, is worthless until he dies.) *Some rich people are worth more dead than alive.*

672. EL ROSARIO al cuello y el diablo en el cuerpo. (The rosary about one's neck and the devil in one's heart.) *A commentary on hypocrites.*

673. EL SARTEN llama a lo olla tiznada. (The frying pan calls the pot black.) *The pot calling the kettle black.*

674. EL SORDO no oye, pero compone. (The deaf can't hear, but they piece things together.) *Reproaches people for not listening carefully and repeating the facts in a fragmentary fashion.*

675. EL TIEMPO causa olvido. (Time causes forgetfulness.) *Out of sight, out of mind.*

676. EL TIEMPO CURA al enfermo, no el ungüento que le embarran. (Time cures the patient, not the ointment applied.) *Time is the best healer.*

677. EL TIEMPO DA consejos. (Time gives advice.) *Experience is the best teacher.*

678. EL TIEMPO desengaña. (Time removes doubt.) *Time will tell.*

679. EL TIEMPO es gran médico. (Time is a great physician.) *Time is the best healer.*

680. EL TIEMPO es oro. (Time is gold.) *Time is money.*

681. EL TIEMPO PERDIDO, los ángeles lo lloran. (Time wasted is mourned by the angels.) *Time is money.*

682. EL TRABAJO de los niños es poco y el que no lo aprovecha es loco. (Children don't work much, and he who does not cultivate it is crazy.) *Comments on the value of children's help.*

683. EL TRABAJO hace la vida agradable. (Work makes life pleasant.) *Recommends work in enjoying life.*

684. EL TRAJE no hace al monje. (Clothes do not make the monk.) *Appearances are deceiving.*

685. EL VIEJO que se cura, cien años dura. (The old one who takes care of himself lives a hundred years.) *Recommends taking care of oneself while one is young to reach a ripe old age.*

686. **EMBORRACHA al hombre si lo quieres conocer.** (Get the man drunk if you want to get to know him.) *Drunks have loose tongues.*

687. **EN ARBOL caído todos suben a las ramas.** (Everyone climbs the branches of a fallen tree.) *Fallen pride inspires contempt.*

688. **EN ARCA abierta, el justo peca.** (An open chest tempts the pious.) *Opportunity makes the thief.*

689. **EN BOCA cerrada no entran moscas.** (No flies get into a closed mouth.) *Silence is golden.*

690. **EN BOCA del discreto, lo público es secreto.** (In the mouth of the discreet, what people say is a secret.) *A prudent man keeps secrets to himself.*

691. **EN BOCA DEL MENTIROSO, lo cierto se hace dudoso.** (In the mouth of a liar, the truth becomes doubtful.) *Truth becomes doubtful when uttered by a liar.*

692. **EN CADA CASA se cuecen habas.** (Horse beans are cooked in every home.) *All people have faults, but we should look first at our own.*

693. **EN CAMA angosta, métete en medio.** (In a narrow bed, get in the middle.) *Suggests we make the best of a bad situation.*

694. **EN CASA del herrero todos son herreros.** (At the blacksmith's, everyone is a smith.) *Members of a family acquire the characteristics of the parents.*

695. **EN CASA DEL 'HORCADO no se habla de *cabresto*.** (Mention not the rope in the home of one who has been hanged.) *Suggests that we avoid hurting people's feelings.*

696. **EN CASA DEL JABONERO el que no cae, resbala.** (At the soapmaker's, he who doesn't fall will slip.) *We should not criticize defects in others, lest we have them ourselves.*

697. **EN CASA DEL ZAPATERO, los zapatos de palo.** (At the shoemaker's, everyone wears wooden shoes.) *In the shoemaker's house, no one wears shoes.*

698. **EN CASA DE MUSICO todos son músicos.** (At the musician's everyone's a musician.) *Members of a family acquire the same characteristics.*

699. **EN CASA DE RICA, ella manda y ella grita.** (At the home of the rich woman, she shouts and gives the orders.) *The rich wife holds the reins in the household.*

700. **EN CASA DE TIA, pero no cada día.** (Visit your aunt, but not every day.) *Advice against becoming pests with our visits.*

701. **EN CASA LLENA pronto se cena.** (When the larder is full, people eat right away.) *With an abundance of means, one can easily accomplish things.*

702. **EN CASA LLENA pronto se guisa la cena.** (When the larder is full, supper's quickly prepared.) *With resources, one can overcome most difficulties.*

703. **EN CASA SIN HARINA, todo se vuelve una *muina*.** (In a home without flour, everything becomes an annoyance.) *When poverty comes in at the door, love flies out the window.*

704. **EN COJERA de perro y lágrimas de mujer, no hay que creer.** (Do not believe a dog's limp or a woman's tears.) *Advice against being impressed by exaggerated lamentations.*

705. **EN CORRAL ajeno la vaca cuerna al buey.** (In a strange corral the cow gores the ox.) *Suggests that people suffer hardships in strange surroundings.*

706. **EN EL DEDO malo son todos los *trompezones*.** (All blows fall on the sore toe.) *Misfortunes never come singly.*

707. **EN EL MEJOR PAÑO cae la mancha.** (The stain falls on the best cloth.) *It happens in the best of families.*

708. **EN EL MODO de cortar el queso se conoce el que es tendero.** (The storekeeper shows he is a storekeeper in the way he cuts cheese.) *A craftsman shows how good he is by the way he handles his tools.*

709. **EN LA TARDANZA está el peligro.** (The danger lies in the delay.) *He who hesitates is lost.*

61

710. **ENFERMO que caga y mea, el diablo que se lo crea.** (If the patient moves his bowels and urinates normally, let the devil believe that he is really sick.) *Chides those who pretend to be sick.*

711. **EN LA CARCEL y en la cama se conocen los amigos.** (Friends prove themselves in jail or in illness.) *Adversity is the touchstone of friendship.*

712. **EN LA PUERTA del horno se quema el pan.** (Bread burns at the door of the oven.) *There's many a slip 'twixt the cup and the lip.*

713. **EN LA TIERRA del ciego el tuerto es rey.** (In the land of the blind the one-eyed is king.) *He who has little learning is considered educated among the ignorant.*

714. **EN LO AJENO siempre cae la desgracia.** (Misfortune always falls on things that we have borrowed.) *Advice against borrowing things.*

715. **EN LOS NIDOS de antaño no hay pájaros hogaño.** (There are no birds today in last year's nests.) *Times change and we change with them.*

716. **EN MARTES, ni te cases ni te embarques.** (Do not marry or go on a journey on Tuesday.) *In Spanish, Tuesday is unlucky like Friday the 13th in English.*

717. **EN NOMBRANDO al rey de Roma y por la puerta se asoma.** (Speak of the king of Rome and he appears at the door.) *Speaking of the devil and he appears.*

718. **EN PLEITOS de hermanos no metas las manos.** (Don't stick your hands in brothers' quarrels.) *Don't meddle in family affairs.*

719. **EN PUERTA cerrada, el diablo se vuelve.** (The devil turns from a closed door.) *Take away the temptation and avoid the sin.*

720. **EN TIEMPOS de higos, no hay amigos.** (When figs are ready to pick there are no friends.) *Friends are tested in adversity.*

721. **EN TODAS PARTES se cuecen habas.** (Horse beans are cooked in every home.) *Everyone has his faults, and we should look first at our own.*

722. ENTRE AMIGOS honrados, cumplimientos dispensados. (Among close friends, one skips formality.) *Formality is not necessary among close friends.*

723. ENTRE AMIGO Y AMIGO: un fiscal y dos testigos. (Between one friend and another, a lawyer and two witnesses.) *Business is business.*

724. ENTRE COL y col, lechugas. (Heads of lettuce among the cabbage.) *Advice in favor of taking the bad with the good.*

725. ENTRE DOS AMIGOS, un notario y dos testigos. (Between two friends, a notary and two witnesses.) *Business is business.*

726. ENTRE LAS GENTES hay mil gustos diferentes. (There are a thousand different tastes from one person to another.) *Everyone to his taste.*

727. ENTRE LO DICHO y lo hecho hay un gran trecho. (There's a great difference between what is said and what is done.) *It's easier said than done.*

728. ENTRE LOS PARIENTES y el sol, entre más lejos, mejor. (With the sun and one's relatives, the farther away the better.) *Recommends not getting too close to one's relatives.*

729. ENTRE MARIDO y mujer, nadie se debe meter. (No one should meddle in quarrels between husband and wife.) *Between husband and wife, no one should interfere.*

730. ENTRE MAS ALTA la subida, más alta la caída. (The higher the climb, the higher the fall.) *The higher they climb, the harder they fall.*

731. ENTRE MAS AMISTAD, más claridad. (The greater the friendship, the more need for frankness.) *Stronger friendship, more clarity.*

732. ENTRE MAS BOTONES, más ojales. (The more buttons the more buttonholes.) *The greater the need, the more resources needed.*

733. ENTRE MAS HONORES, más dolores. (More honors, more worries.) *The greater the glory, the greater the worry.*

63

734. ENTRE MAS SE EMPINA uno, más le ven las nalgas. (The more you bend over, the more your butt will show.) *The more you give in, the more people will take advantage of you.*

735. ENTRE MAS VIEJO, más pendejo. (The older a person gets, the more stupid he becomes.) *The older you get, the stupider you get.*

736. ENTRE MENOS BURROS, más olotes. (The fewer the donkeys, the more the corn.) *The smaller the company, the greater the feast.*

737. EN TU CASA sardina y en la ajena gallina. (Sardines at home and chicken at the neighbor's.) *Censures people who do not eat well at home but eat like kings when they're invited out.*

738. EN TU SALUD lo hallarás. (You'll discover that it is detrimental to your health.) *When we behave inappropriately we're only hurting ourselves.*

739. EN TUS APUROS y afanes, acude a los refranes. (In your needs and toils, resort to your proverbs.) *People often find solutions to their problems in the wisdom of their proverbs.*

740. ES BUENO el encaje, pero no tan ancho. (The lace is all right, but it's too wide.) *Too much of a good thing is not good.*

741. ES LO MISMO LLEGAR a tiempo que ser convidado. (It's just the same to arrive on time as to be invited.) *Said by people who drop in on others just as they are eating, having a party or meeting, etc.*

742. ES MAS EL RUIDO que las nueces. (The noise is more than the pecans.) *Much ado about nothing.*

743. ESTAN MAS CERCA mis dientes que mis parientes. (My teeth are closer than my relatives.) *Said by selfish persons who will eat something they could very well take home to their families.*

744. ESTIRAN MAS TETAS que carretas. (Women's breasts have more influence than ox carts.) *Women have a strong influence on men.*

Fierro caliente, batirlo de repente.
Strike while the iron is hot.

745. **FAVOR OFRECIDO, compromiso contraído.** (A favor offered, an obligation contracted.) *A simple offer to do a favor constitutes a commitment.*

746. **FAVOR PUBLICADO, favor deshonrado.** (A favor made public is a favor without honor.) *A favor loses its value when everyone knows it was done.*

747. **FAVOR REFERIDO, ni de Dios ni del diablo agradecido.** (A favor that is brought up repeatedly is not appreciated.) *No one appreciates being reminded of a favor done for them.*

748. **FEBRERO loco, marzo otro poco.** (February is unstable and March a bit too.) *A comment on the instability of the weather during February and March.*

749. **FIERRO CALIENTE, batirlo de repente.** (A hot piece of iron must be beaten immediately.) *Strike while the iron is hot.*

750. **FIERRO MOVEDIZO no cría *mojo*.** (A moving piece of iron does not get rusty.) *A rolling stone gathers no moss.*

751. **FILO de hacha corta pino, no hocico de coyotino.** (The edge of the axe, not the mouth of the coyote, will cut the pine tree.) *Actions speak louder than words.*

65

752. **FLOR marchita y fe perdida, nunca vuelven a la vida.** (A withered flower and a lost faith never return to life.) *It's easier to lose faith than to find it again.*

753. **FONDO salido, busca marido.** (A slip that's showing looks for a husband.) *Said to a woman whose slip is showing.*

754. **FORTUNA mal adquirida nunca prospera.** (Ill-gotten fortune will never prosper.) *Fortune ill acquired never prospers.*

755. **FRAILE que pide pan toma carne si se la dan.** (The friar that asks for bread will take meat if it is offered to him.) *Beggars can't be choosers.*

756. **FRAILE que pide por Dios, pide siempre para dos.** (The friar that asks in the name of God asks for two.) *Mendicants ask for themselves and pray for the soul of the donor.*

757. **FRAY Modesto nunca llegó a prior.** (Friar Modest never became prior.) *Faint heart never won fair lady.*

758. **FUISTE FIADOR, serás pagador.** (You were the bondsman, you'll be the payer.) *Advice against co-signing or offering bond for others.*

Gato encogido, brinco seguro.
A cat that's crouched is ready to jump.

759. GALLINA come huevos, más que le quemen el pico.
(The hen that eats her eggs will continue even though
you burn her beak.) *Bad habits are hard to break.*

760. GALLINA que come huevos, aunque le quemen el pico.
(The hen that eats her eggs will continue even though
you burn her beak.) *Bad habits are hard to break.*

**761. GALLINA que da en comer huevos, aunque le corten
el pico.** (The hen that makes it a habit to eat her eggs
will continue even though you may cut off her beak.)
Bad habits are hard to break.

762. GALLINA VIEJA hace buen caldo. (An old hen makes
good soup.) *Old maids make good lovers.*

763. GALLO, caballo y mujer, por su raza has de conocer.
(A rooster, a horse, and a woman must be chosen for
their class.) *Advice on choosing one's wife.*

764. GANAR UNO y gastar dos, no tiene perdón de Dios.
(To earn one dollar and spend two has no forgiveness
from God.) *Censures the spendthrift.*

765. GANE mi gallo y aunque sea rabón. (My rooster, tail-
less or not, has to win.) *An observation that some people
have to win.*

766. GARAÑON que no relincha, que lo capen. (The stallion that does not neigh should be castrated.) *Recommends getting rid of a worker who does not perform.*

767. GATO CON GUANTES no pesca ratones. (A cat wearing gloves catches no mice.) *Suggests using the right clothes, tools, etc., to do a particular job.*

768. GATO ENCOGIDO, brinco seguro. (A cat that's crouched is ready to jump.) *The lull before the storm.*

769. GATO ENGUANTADO no pesca ratón. (A cat wearing gloves will catch no mice.) *Suggests using the right clothes, tools, etc., to do a particular job.*

770. GATO ESCALDADO del agua fría huye. (The scalded cat flees from cold water.) *The burnt child dreads the fire.*

771. GATO LLORON no pesca ratón. (A mewing cat catches no mice.) *Great talkers are little doers.*

772. GATO QUE DUERME no caza ratón. (The cat that sleeps catches no mice.) *Don't let the grass grow under your feet.*

773. GATO TODO enguantado no caza ratón. (A cat wearing gloves catches no mice.) *Suggests using the right clothes, tools, etc., to do a particular job.*

774. GENIO y figura, hasta la sepultura. (Face and figure from birth to the grave.) *What's bred in the bone will never come out of the flesh.*

775. GLORIA vana florece pero no grana. (Vainglory blooms but it never seeds.) *All is vanity.*

776. GOTA a gota la mar se apoca. (Drop by drop the sea lessens.) *Slow but sure.*

777. GOTA por gota el balde se llena. (Drop by drop the bucket is filled.) *Slow but sure. He who perseveres goes far.*

778. GOZA DE ABRIL y mayo, que agosto ya llegará. (Enjoy April and May, for August will surely come.) *Gather ye rosebuds while ye may.*

68

779. **GOZA DE TU POCO mientras busca más el loco.** (Enjoy what little you have while the madman looks for more.) *Be content with what you have.*

780. **GRACIA es andar entre las llamas y no quemarse.** (The trick is to walk among the flames and not get burned.) *Comments on the importance of playing with fire and not getting burned.*

781. **GRANDE, aunque sea hueso.** (Let it be large, even though it be all bone.) *Chides those who prefer quantity over quality.*

782. **GUARDA LOS CENTAVOS que los pesos llegarán.** (Save the pennies and the dollars will come.) *Take care of your pennies and the dollars will take care of themselves.*

783. **GUARDATE DE HOMBRE que no habla y de perro que no ladra.** (Beware a quiet man and a silent dog.) *Still waters run deep.*

784. **GUARDATE DEL AGUA mansa.** (Beware of still waters.) *Still waters run deep.*

785. **GUSTO con gusto, siempre es gusto.** (Pleasure with taste is always a pleasure.) *It's always a pleasure to choose one's pleasure with good taste.*

Hay que bailar al son que nos toquen.
One must dance to the tune that is played.

786. **HABIENDO CARNE y cueva, aunque llueva.** (As long as there is meat and a cave, let it rain.) *As long as one has food and shelter, the rest is not important.*

787. **HABLANDO DEL REY de Roma y él a la puerta se asoma.** (Speak of the king of Rome and he appears at the door.) *Speaking of the devil and he appears.*

788. **HABLANDO DEL RUIN de Roma y él por la puerta se asoma.** (Speak of the devil and he appears at the door.) *Speaking of the devil and he appears.*

789. **HABLANDO, la gente se entiende.** (People understand one another by talking.) *Suggests communication as a means to solving people's problems.*

790. **HABLEN CARTAS y callen barbas.** (Let the documents speak and the beards keep quiet.) *Documentary evidence is better than oral statements.*

791. **HABLO el buey y dijo mu.** (The ox spoke and he said "moo.") *A fool opens his mouth only to put his foot in it.*

792. **HACER BIEN nunca se pierde.** (Doing good is never lost.) *Good deeds are never lost.*

793. **HACER CARAVANA con sombrero ajeno.** (To greet peo-

ple with someone else's hat in one's hand.) *To claim ownership for someone else's thoughts or opinions.*

794. **HACER DE TRIPAS corazón.** (To pluck up courage from one's intestines.) *To make the best of a bad situation.*

795. **HACERLE BIEN al ingrato es lo mismo que ofenderlo.** (Doing a good turn to an ingrate is the same as offending him.) *Not everyone appreciates kindness.*

796. **HACER UNA VIDA y dos mandados.** (To make one life and two errands.) *To kill two birds with one stone.*

797. **HACES MAL, espera otro tal.** (If you do wrong, expect wrong.) *As you sow, so shall you reap.*

798. **HACIENDO por la vida, que la muerte sola llega.** (I'm trying to live, for death comes by itself.) *A polite way of saying one's minding his own business.*

799. **HACIENDOSE el milagro, aunque lo haga el diablo.** (Let the miracle be performed, even if the devil performs it.) *The importance of an achievement is that it gets done.*

800. **HAGASE el milagro, aunque lo haga el diablo.** (Let the miracle be performed, even if the devil performs it.) *The importance of an achievement is that it gets done.*

801. **HARE COMO EL INDIO—Ya comí, ya me voy.** (I'll do as the Indian said, "I've eaten, I'm leaving.") *Censures those who desert their friends, once no more favors are forthcoming.*

802. **HARTO AYUDA el que no estorba.** (It would be helpful if you didn't get in the way.) *A hint to get a person to move or to get out of the way.*

803. **HARTO AYUNA el que mal come.** (He fasts sufficiently who eats badly.) *Suggests that the poor are in no position to make further sacrifices.*

804. **¡HASTA LOS GATOS quieren zapatos!** (Even cats want to wear shoes!) *His claims are greater than what he deserves.*

805. **HASTA QUE no lo veas, no lo creas.** (Don't believe it until you see it.) *Seeing is believing.*

806. HAY GUSTOS de gustos. (There are tastes even among tastes.) *There is no accounting for tastes.*

807. HAY GUSTOS que merecen palos. (There are tastes that deserve a beating.) *Criticizes people for their bad taste.*

808. HAY MUERTOS que no hacen ruido y son mayores sus penas. (There are dead that make no noise and their troubles are worse.) *We all have our troubles and there's no reason to complain too much.*

809. HAY MUY POCO que escoger entre las podridas. (There is small choice among the rotten.) *Suggests that there's not much of a selection.*

810. HAY QUE BAILAR al son que nos toquen. (One must dance to the tune that is played.) *One must act according to circumstances.*

811. HAY QUE DORMIR y trabajar para avanzar. (One must sleep and work in order to prosper.) *Early to bed and early to rise makes a man healthy, wealthy, and wise.*

812. HAY QUE SABER perder antes de aprender a jugar. (One must learn to lose before he learns to play.) *Advice against being poor losers.*

813. HAY QUE TOMAR lo bueno con lo malo. (One must take the good with the bad.) *Suggests one accept the bad along with the good.*

814. HAY QUIEN mucho cacarea y no pone nunca un huevo. (There are many who cackle and have never laid an egg.) *Censures those who pretend to be worth more than they really are.*

815. HAY REMEDIO contra todo, menos contra la muerte. (There's a remedy for everything except for death.) *There's no getting around death.*

816. HAY VECES que vale más ser gallina que gallo. (Sometimes it is better to be a chicken than a rooster.) *Discretion is the better part of valor.*

817. HAZ BIEN y no acates a quién. (Do good and mind not to whom.) *Charity is its own reward.*

818. **HAZ BIEN y no mires a quién.** (Do good and mind not to whom.) *Disinterest is the noblest part of kindness.*

819. **HAZ LA NOCHE, noche y el día, día.** (Make night out of night and day out of day.) *Live life as it should be lived—normally.*

820. **HAZ MAL y espera otro tal.** (Do wrong and expect equal wrong.) *As you sow, so shall you reap.*

821. **HAZTE EL TONTO y come con las dos manos.** (Pretend to be a fool and eat heartily.) *Live your life and do not mind the world.*

822. **HAZTE SORDO y ponte gordo.** (Pretend to be deaf and get fat.) *Recommends facing life with indifference.*

823. **HAZTE VIEJO temprano y vivirás sano.** (Become old early in life and you will live sanely.) *Those who would be young when they are old must be old when they are young.*

824. **HERMANOS y gatos, todos son ingratos.** (Relatives and cats are all ungrateful.) *Suggests that relatives are unappreciative.*

825. **HIJO de bien, siempre lo ven.** (A nice person is always welcome.) *A person who has good manners is accepted everywhere.*

826. **HIJO DE GATA, come ratón.** (The son of the cat eats mice.) *Like father, like son.*

827. **HIJO DE GATA, ratones mata.** (The son of the cat kills mice.) *Like father, like son.*

828. **HIJO ERES y padre serás.** (You are a son and a father you shall be.) *As you treat your parents, your children will treat you.*

829. **HIJOS CRECIDOS, trabajos llovidos.** (Grown children bring their parents a downpour of worries.) *Parents' worries increase as their children grow up.*

830. **HIJO SIN DOLOR, madre sin amor.** (A child without pain, a mother without love.) *People care little for that which costs them little.*

831. HIJOS NO TENEMOS y nombres les ponemos. (We have no children and yet have given them names.) *Don't count your chickens before they are hatched.*

832. HOMBRE CASADO, siempre desconfiado. (Married man, always untrusting.) *A married man is always distrustful.*

833. HOMBRE DE BIEN, siempre lo ven. (An honest man is always welcome.) *A person with good manners is accepted everywhere.*

834. HOMBRE HONRADO, primero muerto que injuriado. (A man of honor prefers death to dishonor.) *Honor at any cost.*

835. HOMBRE PREVENIDO nunca fue vencido. (A man who is prepared will never be vanquished.) *Forewarned is forearmed.*

836. HONOR y provecho no caben en un mismo lecho. (Honor and gain do not fit in the same bed.) *Honor and profit are no bedfellows.*

837. HONRA y provecho no caben en un mismo saco. (Honor and profit cannot be contained in the same bag.) *One cannot both be honest and make a profit.*

838. HOY POR TI, mañana por mí. (Today for you, tomorrow for me.) *One good turn deserves another.*

839. HOY P' UNOS y mañana p' otros. (Today for some, tomorrow for others.) *Some die today, others tomorrow.*

840. HOY SON LOS AMORES y mañana los desengaños. (Love today, disappointment tomorrow.) *Today there's love, tomorrow disillusion.*

841. HUMANO es el errar, divino el perdonar. (To err is human, to forgive, divine.) *Easy to make mistakes, harder to forgive.*

842. HUMO y mala cara sacan la gente de casa. (Smoke and a gloomy face chase people from your house.) *An unpleasant disposition makes people feel unwelcome.*

Ir por lana y volver trasquilado.
To go for wool and come back shorn.

843. **INDIO, pájaro y conejo no metas en tu casa aunque te mueras de viejo.** (Accept not in your home an Indian, a bird, or a rabbit even if you're dying of old age.) *Expresses colonial feeling that Indians were untrustworthy.*

844. **INDIO que suspira no llega a su tierra.** (The Indian that sighs never gets back home.) *This is said to or about a person when he sighs in the presence of others.*

845. **IRA de hermanos, ira de diablos.** (The ire of brothers is the ire of the devil.) *No quarrels are so fierce as those between relatives.*

846. **IR por lana y volver trasquilado.** (To go for wool and come back shorn.) *Said of a person who sets out to accomplish some task, fails, and returns in embarrassment.*

Júntate con los buenos y serás uno de ellos.
Keep company with good people and you
will be one of them.

847. **JUGANDO, jugando, nace un niño llorando.** (In play
and in fun, a child can be born.) *Warns that even playing
at love can have serious consequences.*

848. **JUNTATE con los buenos y serás uno de ellos.** (Keep
company with good people and you will be one of
them.) *Recommends that you watch the company you
keep.*

Los muertos no hablan.
The dead do not talk.

849. **LA AMBICION del dinero hace al hombre pecador.** (The desire to have money makes a sinner out of man.) *The love of money is the root of all evil.*

850. **LA AUSENCIA borra los recuerdos.** (Absence erases all memories.) *Out of sight, out of mind.*

851. **LA AUSENCIA causa olvido.** (Absence causes forgetfulness.) *Out of sight, out of mind.*

852. **LA AUSENCIA para el amor**
es lo que el aire *pal* fuego;
si es chica se apaga luego
si es grande arde mejor.

(Absence is to love
What air is to the fire;
If it is small, it goes out soon;
If it is great, it burns stronger.)

Absence makes the heart grow fonder.

853. **LA BUENA CAPA todo lo tapa.** (A good cape covers it all.) *Appearances are deceiving.*

854. **LA BURRA no era arisca, los palos la hicieron.** (The donkey was not skittish; she is now because of the beatings she got.) *Bad experiences cause a fearful attitude.*

77

855. **LA CABRA siempre tira al monte (y el indio a lo colorado).** (The goat always heads toward the woods—and the Indian goes for red things.) *What is bred in the bone will never come out of the flesh.*

856. **LA CANA engaña, el diente miente; la arruga desengaña y el pelo en la oreja ni duda deja.** (Gray hairs deceive, the teeth lie; wrinkles leave no doubt and neither does hair in one's ear.) *Wrinkles and hair in one's ear betray one's age.*

857. **LA CANA engaña, el diente miente y la arruga saca de duda.** (Gray hairs deceive, the teeth lie, and one's wrinkles leave no doubt.) *Wrinkles show one's age.*

858. **LA CARA es el espejo del alma.** (The face is the mirror of the soul.) *Facial expressions betray one's feelings.*

859. **LA CARA guarda la honra.** (The face saves the honor.) *An ugly woman is safe from dishonor.*

860. **LA CARIDAD bien ordenada empieza por uno mismo.** (Charity begins with oneself.) *Charity begins at home.*

861. **LA CARNE pegada al hueso es la más sabrosa.** (The meat next to the bone has the best taste.) *Belief that thin women are the most appetizing.*

862. **LA CASADA le pide a la viuda.** (The married woman asks for help from the widow.) *Censures those who ask help of those who need help worse than they do.*

863. **LA CASA quemada, acudir con el agua.** (After the house is burnt, run to it with the water.) *Closing the barn door after the horse is stolen.*

864. **LA CASCARA guarda al palo.** (The bark protects the tree.) *Satirizes people who bathe only once in a blue moon.*

865. **LA COBIJA y la mujer, suavecitas han de ser.** (Blankets and women must be nice and soft.) *A preference for fine, well-mannered women.*

866. **LA COCHINA más flaca es la que quiebra el chiquero.** (The scrawniest sow is the one that breaks down the pigpen.) *The least worthy are the ones that bother the most.*

867. **LA CODICIA rompe el saco.** (Covetousness rips the bag.) *All covet, all lose.*

868. **LA CONDICION hace al ladrón.** (Condition makes the thief.) *Opportunity makes the thief.*

869. **LA CONFIANZA mata al hombre.** (Confidence kills the man.) *Advice against being overconfident.*

870. **LA CONSTANCIA hace milagros.** (Constancy performs miracles.) *He who hangs on, wins.*

871. **LA COSTUMBRE hace ley.** (Custom makes law.) *Many laws are based on the customs of people.*

872. **LA CRUZ en el pecho y el diablo en los hechos.** (The cross on the breast and the devil in his actions.) *Angel in appearance, devil in deed.*

873. **LA CUÑA, para que apriete, ha de ser del mismo palo.** (The wedge, to be effective, must come from the same wood.) *No worse enemy than a former friend.*

874. **LA DIETA cura más que la lanceta.** (Diet cures more than the lancet.) *An ounce of prevention is worth a pound of cure.*

875. **LA DILIGENCIA es madre de la buena ventura.** (Diligence is the mother of good fortune.) *To have anything one must work hard.*

876. **LADRON que roba a ladrón no tiene salvación.** (The thief that steals from a thief has no salvation.) *A hardened criminal cannot be rehabilitated.*

877. **LADRON que roba a ladrón tiene cien años de perdón y otros tantos de condenación.** (A thief who steals from another thief earns a hundred years' pardon and as many more of condemnation.) *It isn't so bad for one thief to steal from another, yet a thief is a thief and should be condemned.*

878. **LA ESCOBA nueva barre muy bien.** (A new broom sweeps very well.) *New things are appreciated until the novelty wears off.*

879. **LA ESPERANZA es la última que muere.** (Hope is the last thing that dies.) *While there's life, there's hope.*

880. **LA EXPERIENCIA es madre de la ciencia.** (Experience is the mother of science.) *A belief that experience helps the work of the scientist.*

881. **LA FAMILIARIDAD crea desprecio.** (Familiarity breeds contempt.) *Familiarity breeds contempt.*

882. **LA FLOJERA es madre de la pobreza.** (Laziness is the mother of poverty.) *People will not get ahead as long as they are lazy.*

883. **LA FRUTA prohibida es la más apetecida.** (Forbidden fruit is the tastiest.) *Forbidden fruit is sweetest.*

884. **LA GALLINA de mi vecina está más gorda que la mía.** (My neighbor's hen is fatter than my own.) *The grass is always greener on the other side of the fence.*

885. **LA GENTE hablando se entiende.** (People understand one another by talking.) *Recommends discussion as a means to solve people's problems.*

886. **LAGUNA que no tiene desagüe tiene resumidero.** (The lake with no outlet has a drain.) *A spendthrift, no matter how much he may earn, will let his money slip through his fingers.*

887. **LA HONRADEZ es la mejor política.** (Honor is the best policy.) *Honesty is the best policy.*

888. **LA LENGUA guarda al pescuezo.** (The tongue protects the neck.) *Advice against loose talk.*

889. **LA LETRA con sangre entra.** (Letters penetrate with blood.) *Spare the rod and spoil the child.*

890. **LA LEY de Caifás: al amolado, amolarlo más.** (The Law of Caifas: the downtrodden, trample them some more.) *Some people take advantage of the unfortunate.*

891. **LA LIMPIEZA es el lujo del pobre.** (Cleanliness is the luxury of the poor man.) *The very poor have no means to afford being clean.*

892. **LA LUCHA se hace, la suerte es la mala.** (The attempt

is made; it's one's fate that's bad.) *No matter how hard one tries to do a thing, it seems fate spoils our plans.*

893. **LA MANCHA de la mora con otra verde se quita.** (The stain of the mulberry is taken off with a green mulberry.) *There is always a way out of a bad situation.*

894. **LA MEJOR SALSA es el hambre.** (The best sauce is hunger.) *Hunger is the best sauce.*

895. **LA MEJOR SUEGRA, vestida de negra.** (The best mother-in-law is the one dressed in black.) *A dead mother-in-law is the best mother-in-law.*

896. **LA MEJOR VENGANZA es olvidar la injuria.** (The noblest vengeance is to forget the injury.) *The noblest revenge is to forgive the wrong.*

897. **LA MENTIRA dura mientras la verdad llega.** (A lie lasts only until the truth arrives.) *A lie will be found out.*

898. **LA MENTIRA es como el maíz: sola sale.** (A lie is like corn: it crops out by itself.) *A lie will come out in due time.*

899. **LA MENTIRA es hija del diablo; la verdad es hija de Dios.** (A lie is the daughter of the devil; truth is the daughter of God.) *A lie is the devil's offspring; truth is the child of God.*

900. **LA MENTIRA presto es vencida.** (A lie is soon vanquished.) *A liar is soon found out.*

901. **LA MIERDA, entre más le escarban, mas *jiede*.** (The more you scratch excrement, the more it stinks.) *A shady affair becomes worse with probing.*

902. **LA MISA, dígala el cura.** (Let the priest say Mass.) *If you want a thing done well, call an expert.*

903. **LA MONA, aunque se vista de seda, mona se queda.** (Dress a monkey in finest silk, it still remains a monkey.) *Dress a monkey as you will, it remains a monkey still.*

904. **LA MUCHA CORRELACION es causa de menosprecio.** (Much correlation causes scorn.) *Familiarity breeds contempt.*

905. **LA MUJER alta y delgada y la yegua colorada.** (The woman must be tall and slender and the mare sorrel colored.) *A personal preference for tall, slender women.*

906. **LA MUJER CASADA, preñada y en casa.** (The married woman should be gotten pregnant and kept at home.) *A married woman's place is in the home.*

907. **LA MUJER QUE ES HONRADA, mas que ande entre la bola.** (An honest woman will remain honest even though she may keep bad company.) *A belief that a good woman will be good regardless of her environment.*

908. **LA MUJER Y EL VIDRIO siempre corren peligro.** (Women and glass are always in danger.) *A woman's virtue and a piece of glass are fragile.*

909. **LA MUJER Y LA SARDINA, entre más chica, más fina.** (Women and sardines, the smaller the finer.) *A personal preference for small women.*

910. **LA MUJER Y LAS TORTILLAS, calientes han de ser.** (Women and tortillas should be hot.) *A personal preference for passionate women.*

911. **LA MULA es mula y cuando no patea recula.** (The mule is a mule, and when she doesn't kick she will rear.) *Fools and the stubborn act accordingly.*

912. **LA NECESIDAD carece de ley.** (Necessity lacks law.) *Necessity respects no law.*

913. **LA NECESIDAD hace a la vieja trotar.** (Necessity makes the old woman trot.) *Necessity is the mother of invention.*

914. **LA NECESIDAD tiene cara de hereje.** (Necessity has a hideous countenance.) *Stern is the visage of necessity.*

915. **LA NOCHE es capa de pecadores.** (Night is the cover of the sinner.) *Suggests that most crimes are committed at night.*

916. **LA OBLIGACION es antes que la devoción.** (Obligation before devotion.) *Duty before pleasure.*

917. **LA OCASION hace al ladrón.** (Occasion makes the thief.) *Opportunity makes the thief.*

82

918. **LA OCASION perdida no se recobra fácil.** (A lost opportunity is never regained.) *There's no making up for a lost opportunity.*

919. **LA OCIOSIDAD es madre de todos los vicios.** (Idleness is the mother of all vices.) *An idle mind is the devil's playground.*

920. **LA ORACION breve sube al cielo.** (A short prayer goes to heaven.) *Brief requests are often granted.*

921. **LA ORACION del padre el hijo la reza.** (The son repeats his father's prayer.) *Like father, like son.*

922. **LA PACIENCIA es amarga pero su fruto es dulce.** (Patience is bitter but its fruit is sweet.) *Patience's reward is sweet.*

923. **LA PEREZA es madre de la pobreza.** (Laziness is the mother of poverty.) *Laziness engenders poverty.*

924. **LA PRACTICA hace al maestro.** (Practice makes the master.) *Practice makes perfect.*

925. **LA PRIMERA MUJER escoba, la segunda, señora.** (The first wife is a slave, the second a lady.) *Suggests better treatment for one's second wife.*

926. **LA QUE COME manzana se cría sana.** (The person who eats apples is healthy.) *An apple a day keeps the doctor away.*

927. **LA QUE DA el pico da el *nico*.** (The girl who kisses doesn't stop at kissing.) *Kissing can have serious consequences.*

928. **LA QUE DE AMARILLO se viste, en su hermosura confía.** (The woman who dresses in yellow is confident of her beauty.) *Not every woman can wear yellow.*

929. **LA QUE SE CASA, en su casa; la soltera, dondequiera.** (The married woman at home; the single girl can go anywhere.) *Shows there is a difference in state between a married woman and a single girl.*

930. **LA RANA más aplastada es la que más recio grita.** (The frog that is the most downtrodden is the one that croaks

the loudest.) *Those who are least important are the ones that complain most.*

931. LA REATA se revienta por lo más delgado. (A rope breaks where it is thinnest.) *A chain is as strong as its weakest link.*

932. LA RISA abunda en la boca de los locos. (Laughter abounds in the mouth of the fool.) *Fools are always laughing to themselves.*

933. LA ROPA limpia no necesita jabón. (Clean clothes need no soap.) *A person who has no blame need not give excuses.*

934. LA ROPA sucia en casa se lava. (Dirty clothes should be washed at home.) *Personal problems should be solved in private.*

935. LA SANGRE sin fuego hierve. (Blood boils without need of fire.) *Blood is thicker than water.*

936. LAS CANAS salen de ganas, la arruga saca de duda. (Gray hair comes out at will; wrinkles betray one's age.) *Wrinkles are a sign of aging.*

937. LAS COSAS claras y el chocolate espeso. (Things clear and cocoa thick.) *Call a spade a spade.*

938. LAS COSAS se parecen a sus dueños. (Things resemble their owners.) *A man's tastes are shown in his possessions.*

939. LAS CUENTAS claras hacen los buenos amigos. (Clear accounts make good friends.) *Advises us to be serious in matters of accounts.*

940. LAS CUENTAS claras y el chocolate espeso. (Accounts in order and the cocoa thick.) *Don't mix business with pleasure.*

941. LAS ENFERMEDADES llegan a caballo y se van a pie. (Illnesses come on horseback and leave on foot.) *Illnesses are not cured overnight.*

942. LAS ESPERANZAS engordan pero no mantienen. (Hope fattens but it doesn't keep you alive.) *Man cannot live on hope alone.*

84

943. **LAS HOJAS en el árbol no duran toda la vida.** (The leaves on a tree do not last forever.) *Everything must end.*

944. **LAS MALAS NUEVAS siempre son ciertas.** (Bad news is always certain.) *Bad news is always true.*

945. **LAS MUJERES hablan mucho y esuchan poco.** (Women talk much and listen little.) *Expresses the belief that women do a lot of talking and little listening.*

946. **LAS NOTICIAS malas tienen alas.** (Bad news has wings.) *Bad news travels fast.*

947. **LAS *PADERES* tienen oídos.** (Walls have ears.) *Little pitchers have big ears.*

948. **LAS PIEDRAS rodando se encuentran.** (Stones meet as they roll along.) *It's a small world.*

949. **LAS SUEGRAS ni de azúcar son buenas.** (Mothers-in-law are no good even when made of sugar.) *A negative appraisal of mothers-in-law.*

950. **LA SUERTE de la fea, la bonita la desea.** (The luck of a homely girl is often coveted by a pretty girl.) *Homely girls are many times more successful at marriage than pretty ones.*

951. **LA TENTACION hace al ladrón.** (Temptation makes the thief.) *Opportunity makes the thief.*

952. **LA VACA es ligera pero la ternera va adelante.** (The cow is fast but the heifer is even faster.) *A bad mother may have a daughter that will turn out to be much worse than she is.*

953. **LA VELA se le enciende al santo que la merece.** (The candle is lit in honor of the saint that deserves it.) *One should know who can help him and give him due credit.*

954. **LA VERDAD, aunque severa, es amiga verdadera.** (The truth, although harsh, is a true friend.) *Recommends that we should favor truth.*

955. **LA VERDAD es amarga.** (Truth is bitter.) *The taste of truth is bitter.*

956. **LA VERDAD es hija de Dios.** (Truth is the daughter of God.) *Truth is divine.*

957. **LA VERDAD es hija de Dios y heredera de su gloria.** (Truth is the daughter of God and an heir to His glory.) *Truth is divine.*

958. **LA VERDAD HUYE de los rincones.** (Truth avoids dark corners.) *Truth never hides in dark corners.*

959. **LA VERDAD NO PECA pero incomoda.** (Truth doesn't sin but it makes one ill at ease.) *The truth can be annoying to some people.*

960. **LA VERDAD PADECE pero no perece.** (Truth suffers but it does not perish.) *Truth will endure.*

961. **LA VIDA de los casados los ángeles la desean.** (Angels envy the life of married couples.) *Considers marriage as a perfect state.*

962. **LA VIRTUD es hermosa en las más feas y el vicio es feo en las más hermosas.** (Virtue is beautiful in the ugliest women and vice is ugly in the most beautiful.) *Contrasts virtue and vice in women.*

963. **LA VIUDA llora y otros cantan en la boda.** (The widow weeps and others sing at the wedding.) *Comments on how fickle life can be.*

964. **LA ZORRA mudará los dientes pero no las mientes.** (The fox may lose its teeth but not its ways.) *The leopard cannot change its spots.*

965. **LA ZORRA nunca se mira la cola.** (The fox never sees her tail.) *It's hard for us to see our own defects.*

966. **LES DAN ALMOHADA y piden colchón.** (One gives them a pillow and they ask for a mattress.) *You give them an inch and they take a mile.*

967. **LES DAN LA MANO y cogen el pie.** (You extend your hand to them and they take your foot.) *You give them an inch and they take a mile.*

968. **LIBRO cerrado no saca letrado.** (A closed book will not make a man learned.) *People have to apply themselves to get ahead.*

969. LIBROS y amigos, raros y buenos. (Books and friends, few and good.) *Suggests being choosy about one's friends.*

970. LLAMAR a Dios de tú. (To address God familiarly.) *Said in reference to the cream of society.*

971. LLEGANDO al campo santo no hay calaveras plateadas. (On reaching the graveyard, there are no gold-plated skulls.) *Death makes equal the high and the low.*

972. LLEGATE a los buenos y serás uno de ellos. (Keep company with good men and you'll be one.) *A man is known by the company he keeps.*

973. LLUVIAS de abril dan a mayo flores mil. (April showers give May a thousand flowers.) *April showers bring May flowers.*

974. LO BARATO cuesta caro. (Cheap things turn out to be expensive.) *A comment on false economy.*

975. LO BIEN HECHO, ni trabajo da venderlo. (What's well made is easily sold.) *Used as a compliment to a beauty who passes by.*

976. LOBOS de la misma camada siempre andan juntos. (Wolves of the same litter are always together.) *Birds of a feather flock together.*

977. LO CORTES no le quita nada a lo valiente. (Courtesy takes nothing away from valor.) *Being gentle does not mean one is a coward.*

978. LO DEL AGUA, al agua. (What comes from the water returns to the water.) *Easy come, easy go.*

979. LO FIADO es pariente de lo dado. (Credit is a relative of that which is given away.) *Advice against selling on credit.*

980. LO *HALLADO* no es robado. (What's found is not stolen.) *Finders keepers, losers weepers.*

981. LO MAL GANADO se lo lleva el diablo. (Ill-gotten gain is taken away by the devil.) *Ill-gotten gain does not prosper.*

982. LO MEJOR de los dados es tirarlos. (The best throw of the dice is to throw them away.) *A suggestion on how to quit gambling with dice.*

983. LO MIO, mío y lo tuyo también mío. (What's mine is mine and what's yours is also mine.) *Censures people who are extremely selfish.*

984. LO MISMO da atrás que en ancas. (It's the same behind as on the rump.) *The difference between "right now" and "right away."*

985. LO MISMO ES A PIE que andando. (It's all the same, going on foot as walking.) *As long as a thing is done, it matters little how it is done.*

986. LO MISMO ES CHILE que *abuja,* todo pica. (It's all the same, the chili and the needle—they both sting.) *Censures those people who confuse an issue, an idea, or an expression.*

987. LO MISMO ES IRSE que *juirse,* que irse sin pedir licencia. (It's all the same, leaving, fleeing, and leaving without asking for permission.) *Censures those who waste time looking for unimportant differences in things.*

988. LO MISMO PECA el que mata la vaca como el que come la pata. (Both sin equally, he who kills the cow and he who eats the beef hock.) *The accomplice is as guilty as the offender.*

989. LO PERDIDO vaya por Dios. (What's lost is lost because God wills it.) *Don't cry over spilt milk.*

990. LO PRESTADO es hermano de lo dado. (What is lent is a brother to that which is given away.) *Recommends not lending things.*

991. LO QUE AL TIEMPO se deja, al tiempo se queda. (What is left to time stays in time.) *Things that are put off are finally forgotten and never done.*

992. LO QUE BIEN se aprende, tarde se olvida. (What is learned well is not easily forgotten.) *What is well learned is not soon forgotten.*

993. LO QUE CON TUS PADRES hicieres, tus hijos harán

contigo. (What you do to your parents your children will do to you.) *Recommends that you treat your parents well so your children will treat you well.*

994. **LO QUE CUESTA poco, se estima menos.** (That which costs less is valued less.) *One appreciates what one works for.*

995. **LO QUE DE NOCHE se hace, de día mal parece.** (What's done at night looks bad by daylight.) *Things done at night show defects by daylight.*

996. **LO QUE DIOS da, para bien será.** (God's intentions must be for one's benefit.) *God knows best.*

997. **LO QUE EL AGUA trae, el agua se lleva.** (What water brings, water carries away.) *Easy come, easy go.*

998. **LO QUE EL LOBO hace, a la loba le place.** (What the wolf does pleases his mate.) *Wives are pleased with their husbands' achievements.*

999. **LO QUE EN EL AGUA viene, en el agua se va.** (What comes by water, goes away by water.) *Easy come, easy go.*

1000. **LO QUE EN EL CORAZON está, a la boca sale.** (What's in the heart is expressed by the mouth.) *Out of the abundance of the heart the mouth speaketh.*

1001. **LO QUE EN LA CALLE no puedas ver, en tu casa lo has de tener.** (What you can't stand seeing in the street you might see in your own home.) *People that live in glass houses shouldn't throw stones.*

1002. **LO QUE ES BUENO para el hígado, no es bueno para el bazo.** (What's good for the liver is not good for the spleen.) *One man's meat is another man's poison.*

1003. **LO QUE ES DE TODOS no es de nadie.** (What belongs to all belongs to no one.) *Everybody's business is nobody's business.*

1004. **LO QUE GRANJEA uno, eso tiene.** (What one gives of oneself, one has.) *As you sow, so shall you reap.*

1005. **LO QUE HACE el mono, hace la mona.** (What the monkey does, his mate imitates.) *Monkey see, monkey do.*

1006. LO QUE HAS de hacer hoy, no lo dejes para mañana. (What you must do today, don't leave for tomorrow.) *Don't leave for tomorrow what you can do today.*

1007. LO QUE HOY se pierde, se gana mañana. (What is lost today is gained tomorrow.) *Win some, lose some.*

1008. LO QUE LA LOBA hace, al lobo le place. (What the she-wolf does pleases her mate.) *Used in reference to a married couple that lives in perfect harmony.*

1009. LO QUE MUCHO VALE, mucho cuesta. (What costs dearly is valued dearly.) *No gains without pains.*

1010. LO QUE NO AHOGA, engorda. (What doesn't choke you will make you fat.) *Advises against wasting food and suggests eating every bit.*

1011. LO QUE NO CUESTA, volvámoslo fiesta. (What costs nothing, let's make into a fiesta.) *Easy come, easy go.*

1012. LO QUE NO SE EMPIFZA no se acaba. (What is not started is never finished.) *Advises against delay in starting a project.*

1013. LO QUE NO SE GASTA en lágrimas se gasta en suspiros. (What is not used in tears is used in sighs.) *People will always have their troubles.*

1014. LO QUE NO SE PUEDE remediar se ha de aguantar. (What one cannot change one must bear.) *Learn to accept what one cannot change.*

1015. LO QUE OTRO SUDA, poco dura. (What someone else earns by the sweat of his brow does not last long.) *People are liable to squander what they did not earn themselves.*

1016. LO QUE PASO, voló. (What happened flew by.) *Let bygones be bygones.*

1017. LO QUE POCO CUESTA, poco se aprecia. (What's low in price is low in value.) *One appreciates what one works for.*

1018. LO QUE PUEDAS hacer hoy, no lo dejes para mañana. (What you can do today, don't leave until tomorrow.) *Don't leave for tomorrow what you can do today.*

90

1019. **LO QUE SE APRENDE en la cuna siempre dura.** (What is learned in the cradle lasts forever.) *Things learned in childhood are always remembered.*

1020. **LO QUE SE HACE de noche, de día aparece.** (What is done in the night shows up in the morning.) *Things done secretly may come to light later.*

1021. **LO QUE SE HA DE HACER TARDE que se haga temprano.** (What must be done should be done early.) *Don't put off for tomorrow what you can do today.*

1022. **LO QUE SIEMBRES recogerás.** (What you plant you shall gather.) *As you sow, so shall you reap.*

1023. **LO QUE TE DIGAN al oído, no repitas a tu marido.** (Don't repeat to your husband what they tell you in your ear.) *Secrets are meant to be kept.*

1024. **LO QUE TE DIO la suerte, no lo tengas por fuerte.** (Don't consider what fortune has brought you as a sign of your worth.) *Don't rely on the strength of something which luck has brought.*

1025. **LO QUE TIENE la olla lo saca la cuchara.** (What the pot contains is brought out by the spoon.) *It is hard to hide one's feelings.*

1026. **LO QUE UNO GRANJEA, eso tiene.** (What one offers of oneself, one has.) *As you sow, so shall you reap.*

1027. **LO QUE VEO con los ojos, con el dedo lo señalo.** (What I see with my eyes I point out with my finger.) *Seeing is believing.*

1028. **LO QUE VIENE volando, volando se va.** (What comes in flying goes out flying.) *Easy come, easy go.*

1029. **LOS CONSEJOS no pedidos los dan los entremetidos.** (Uncalled-for advice is given by meddlers.) *Censures those who are ever ready to give advice to others.*

1030. **LOS CORTOS y los pendejos se conocen desde lejos.** (Shy people and fools are spotted from afar.) *Said in reference to a shy or timid person.*

1031. **LOS DICHOS de los viejitos son evangelios chiquitos.**

91

(The sayings of old men are little gospels.) *Much can be learned from the advice of the old.*

1032. **LOS DINEROS del sacristán, cantando vienen, cantando se van.** (The sexton's money, it comes in with a song and goes out with a song.) *Like a gambler's money: easy come, easy go.*

1033. **LOS DUELOS con pan son menos.** (Troubles are lessened with bread.) *Troubles are tolerable if one is not also poor.*

1034. **LOS ENAMORADOS piensan que todos tienen los ojos tapados.** (Lovers think that everyone has his eyes covered.) *Lovers think the whole world is blindfolded.*

1035. **LOS GOLPES quitan lo tonto o acaban de *ajachamar*.** (Blows will remove one's stupidity or disfigure completely.) *Spare the rod and spoil the child.*

1036. **LOS HIJOS son la riqueza de los pobres.** (Children are the riches of the poor.) *Children are the wealth of the poor.*

1037. **LOS LOCOS y los niños dicen las verdades.** (Madmen and children utter truths.) *Truth can be heard from the mouths of madmen and children.*

1038. **LOS MUCHACHOS y los borrachos dicen las verdades.** (Children and drunks utter truths.) *Truth can be heard from the mouths of drunks and children.*

1039. **LOS MUERTOS no hablan.** (The dead do not talk.) *Dead men tell no tales.*

1040. **LOS NECIOS admiran lo que no comprenden.** (Fools admire what they don't understand.) *Ignorance is bliss.*

1041. **LOS NECIOS y los porfiados hacen ricos a los abogados.** (Fools and the stubborn make lawyers rich.) *Foolish and stubborn people make drawn-out cases for lawyers.*

1042. **LOS NIÑOS y los locos dicen las verdades.** (Children and madmen utter truths.) *Truths can be heard from the mouths of madmen and children.*

1043. **LOS PALOS quitan lo bruto.** (Beatings remove stupidity.) *Spare the rod and spoil the child.*

1044. **LOS PARIENTES y el sol, entre más lejos, mejor.** (Relatives and the sun—the farther away, the better.) *Suggests not living too close to one's relatives.*

1045. **LOS RICOS son como los marranos: hasta que no mueren no rinden.** (The rich are like pigs: they don't yield until they are dead.) *A comment on the stinginess of rich people.*

Más vale pájaro en mano que *cien* volando.
A bird in the hand is worth two in the bush.

1046. MADRE CONSENTIDORA engorda una serpiente. (An indulgent mother fattens a serpent.) *Spare the rod and spoil the child.*

1047. MADRE pía daño cría. (An indulgent mother raises spoiled children.) *Spare the rod and spoil the child.*

1048. MAESTRO de todo, oficial de nada. (Master of all, official of nothing.) *Jack of all trades, master of none.*

1049. MAL de muchos, consuelo de todos. (Misfortune of many, comfort to all.) *Misery loves company.*

1050. MAL HAYA quien mal piense. (Evil to him who thinks evil.) *Evil breeds evil.*

1051. MAL no comunicado, no desechado. (Trouble not told will not disappear.) *Advises us to tell our troubles to others in order to get some relief from them.*

1052. MALO vendrá que bueno no te traerá. (He is really bad who will not bring you some good.) *It's an ill wind that blows nobody good.*

1053. MAL QUE NO TIENE REMEDIO, hay que aguantarlo. (An illness that can't be cured must be endured.) *Illness that has no remedy must be endured.*

1054. MANDALO y hazlo y serás bien servido. (Order it, do it, and you will be well served.) *If you want a thing well done, do it yourself.*

1055. MAÑANA oscura, tarde segura. (Dark morning, a clear afternoon.) *A belief that a cloudy sky in the morning will clear by the afternoon.*

1056. MARIDO que no da y cuchillo que no corta, que se pierdan, poco importa. (A husband that doesn't provide and a knife that doesn't cut—let them get lost, they don't matter.) *Censures the improvident husband.*

1057. MAS CAGA un buey que cien golondrinas. (One ox makes a larger mess than a hundred swallows.) *One influential person does more than a hundred without influence.*

1058. MAS CERCA están mis dientes que mis parientes. (My teeth are closer than my relatives.) *Said by a person who overindulges in food which he doesn't need and could take home to his family.*

1059. MAS DA el duro que el desnudo. (The miser gives more than the naked.) *You can't get blood out of a turnip.*

1060. MAS DA EL QUE TIENE que el que quiere. (He who has gives more than he who wants to give.) *You can't get blood out of a turnip.*

1061. MAS DUELE dedo que uña. (A finger hurts more than a fingernail.) *Blood is thicker than water.*

1062. MAS HACE el que quiere que el que puede. (He who wants to does more than he who can.) *Where there's a will there's a way.*

1063. MAS HACE UNA HORMIGA andando que un buey echado. (A walking ant does more work than an ox that's lying down.) *Don't let the grass grow under your feet.*

1064. MAS MOSCAS se cogen con miel que con hiel. (More flies are caught with honey than with bile.) *A smooth tongue does more than harsh words.*

1065. MAS PODEROSO es el ruego del amigo que el fierro

95

del enemigo. (A friend's entreaty has more power than the sword of the enemy.) *A smooth tongue accomplishes more than a sword.*

1066. **MAS PUEDE maña que fuerza.** (Resourcefulness can accomplish more than brute strength.) *Brain over brawn.*

1067. **MAS SABE el diablo por viejo que por diablo.** (The devil knows more because he is old than because he is the devil.) *Experience is the best teacher.*

1068. **MAS SABE EL LOCO en su casa que el cuerdo en la ajena.** (The madman knows more about his own home than a man in his senses in another's.) *Everyone is the best judge of his own business.*

1069. **MAS SABE EL TONTO preguntar que cien hombres contestar.** (The fool can ask more questions than a hundred men can answer.) *The fool is able to ask more questions than many are able to answer.*

1070. **MAS TIRAN TETAS que carretas.** (Women's breasts have more influence than ox carts.) *Women have a strong influence on men.*

1071. **MAS VALE ALGO que nada.** (Something is better than nothing.) *Half a loaf is better than none. If we can't get what we want, we must be content with what we have.*

1072. **MAS VALE AMIGO cerca que pariente lejos.** (A friend that's near is worth more than a relative that's far away.) *A friend living near us can give more help in an emergency than a relative who lives far away.*

1073. **MAS VALE a quien Dios ayuda que a quien madruga.** (Better him whom God helps than he who rises early.) *Suggests that all our endeavors without God's help are of no avail.*

1074. **MAS VALE ATOLE con gusto que chocolate con susto.** (Better to eat gruel while you're happy than cocoa when you're frightened.) *A life of want that is happy is preferable to an unhappy life of ease.*

1075. MAS VALE ATOLE con risas que chocolate con lágrimas. (Better gruel with laughter than cocoa with tears.) *A life of want that is happy is preferable to an unhappy life of ease.*

1076. MAS VALE BIEN de lejos que mal de cerca. (A good thing at a distance is better than a bad thing nearby.) *Anything worth having is worth working for.*

1077. MAS VALE CAER en gracia que ser gracioso. (Better to please than to be funny.) *Better to win people's favor than to act like a fool to get people to accept us.*

1078. MAS VALE COMPRADO que regalado. (Better bought than received as a gift.) *Paying for a thing frees us from obligation to the donor.*

1079. MAS VAE DOBLARSE que quebrarse. (Better to bend than to break.) *It is better to compromise than to lose out completely.*

1080. MAS VALE EMBORRACHARSE que lidiar con un borracho. (Better to get drunk than to have to deal with a drunk.) *If you can't beat them, join them.*

1081. MAS VALE HORAS antes que minutos después. (It's better to be hours ahead than a few minutes late.) *Recommends that people should be punctual.*

1082. MAS VALE LLEGAR a tiempo que ser convidado. (Better to arrive in the nick of time than to be invited.) *Said by persons who just happen to arrive as a family is sitting down to a meal.*

1083. MAS VALE MALA avenencia que buena sentencia. (A poor agreement is better than a stiff sentence.) *A bad compromise is better than a good lawsuit.*

1084. MAS VALE MALO conocido que bueno por conocer. (Better ill known than good unknown.) *A bird in the hand is worth two in the bush.*

1085. MAS VALE MANCHA en la frente que mancilla en el corazón. (Better a stain on the forehead than a blemish in one's heart.) *A stain on one's forehead can be washed off, but not so a blemish on one's character.*

1086. MAS VALE maña que fuerza. (Resourcefulness can do more than brute strength.) *Brain over brawn.*

1087. MAS VALE MEAR en jarro de hojelata que en bacín de plata. (Better to urinate in a tin can than in a silver basin.) *A life of need with love is preferable to a life of ease with discord.*

1088. MAS VALE MUCHACHO roto que viejo con pantalones. (Better a youth in rags than an old man in fine clothes.) *Preference for life with a young husband.*

1089. MAS VALE ONZA de prudencia que una libra de ciencia. (An ounce of prudence is worth more than a pound of science.) *An ounce of prevention is worth a pound of cure.*

1090. MAS VALE PAJARO en mano que buitre volando. (A bird in the hand is worth more than a buzzard on the wing.) *A bird in the hand is worth two in the bush.*

1091. MAS VALE PAJARO en mano que *cien* volando. (A bird in the hand is worth more than a hundred on the wing.) *A bird in the hand is worth two in the bush.*

1092. MAS VALE PAN con amor que gallina con dolor. (Better bread given with love than chicken given with resentment.) *A life of want that is happy is preferable to a life of ease clouded by discord and unhappiness.*

1093. MAS VALE PASO que dure, que no que apresure. (Better a pace that will last than one that hastens.) *Recommends doing things calmly and slowly to get better results.*

1094. MAS VALE PASO que dure y no trote que canse. (Better a pace that will last than a trot that will tire.) *Recommends doing things calmly and slowly to get good results.*

1095. MAS VALE PEDIR que robar. (Better to ask than to steal.) *Better to stretch your hand than your neck.*

1096. MAS VALE POCO de lo mejor que mucho de lo peor. (Better a little of the best than a lot of the worst.) *Recommends quality over quantity.*

1097. MAS VALE QUE DIGAN—*Juyó,* y no—Murió. (Better to have them say "He ran," than "He died.") *Better a live coward than a dead hero.*

1098. MAS VALE QUE SOBRE que no que falte. (Better too much than not enough.) *An abundance of something is never harmful, whereas a lack of something can be annoying.*

1099. MAS VALE RODEAR que no rodar. (Better to go around than to roll.) *Better to bend than to break.*

1100. MAS VALE SABADO por la tarde que domingo por la mañana. (Better Saturday afternoon than Sunday morning.) *A bird in the hand is worth two in the bush.*

1101. MAS VALE SABER que haber. (Better to have knowledge than wealth.) *A preference for knowledge rather than riches.*

1102. MAS VALE SANO que pagarle al cirujano. (Better to stay healthy than to pay the doctor.) *An apple a day keeps the doctor away.*

1103. MAS VALE SER cabeza de ratón que cola de león. (Better to be the head of a mouse than the tail of a lion.) *Better somebody important in a small enterprise than nobody in a large concern.*

1104. MAS VALE SOLO que mal acompañado. (Better alone than in bad company.) *Advises us to be careful in our choice of companions and to shun bad company.*

1105. MAS VALE SUERTE que dinero. (Better fortune than money.) *Good luck is more valuable than money.*

1106. MAS VALE TARDE que nunca. (Better late than never.) *Better to do something late than to put it off forever.*

1107. MAS VALE UN AMIGO que mil parientes, ellos lejos y el presente. (A friend close by is worth a thousand relatives far away.) *Friends often come to the rescue when relatives do not.*

1108. MAS VALE UN AMIGO que pariente ni primo. (Better a friend than a relative or cousin.) *Friends often come to the rescue when relatives do not.*

1109. MAS VALE UNA YUNTA andando que cien paradas.
(Better a yoke of oxen walking than a hundred standing.) *Better a yoke of oxen working than a hundred idle.*

1110. MAS VALE UN JUDAS de oro que un crucifijo de acero. (A gold Judas is worth more than a steel crucifix.) *Gold has more market value than steel.*

1111. MAS VALE UN PAR DE TETAS que un centenar de carretas. (A pair of breasts have more influence than a hundred ox carts.) *Women have a strong influence on men.*

1112. MAS VALE UN "TOMA" que dos "te daré." (Better to say "Here, take" than two "I'll give you later.") *A bird in the hand is worth two in the bush.*

1113. MAS VALE VECINO cerca que pariente lejos. (Better a neighbor nearby than a relative far off.) *Neighbors can help more in an emergency than a relative that lives far away.*

1114. MAS VALE VERGÜENZA en cara que mancilla en el corazón. (Better shame on one's face than a blemish in one's heart.) *Humiliation is preferable to a blemish in one's character.*

1115. MAS VALE VIEJO conocido que nuevo por conocer. (Better the old acquaintance than the new stranger.) *A bird in the hand is worth two in the bush.*

1116. MAS VEN cuatro ojos que dos. (Four eyes see better than two.) *Two heads are better than one.*

1117. MATRIMONIO de arrancados, fábrica de encuerados. (A marriage between two paupers is a factory of naked children.) *Censures getting married if the couple has no financial means to take care of a family.*

1118. MATRIMONIO Y MORTAJA del cielo bajan. (Marriage and the shroud descend from heaven.) *What will be, will be.*

1119. MEJOR COMIDA de legumbres con amor que buey gordo con dolor. (Better a meal of vegetables with love than a fat ox with resentment.) *A life of want that is happy is preferable to an unhappy life of ease.*

1120. **MEJOR MALO CONOCIDO que bueno por conocer.** (Better a bad acquaintance that you know than a good one to be met.) *A bird in the hand is worth two in the bush.*

1121. **MEJOR PAN DURO que ninguno.** (Better hard bread than none at all.) *Half a loaf is better than none.*

1122. **MENTE sana en cuerpo sano.** (A sound mind in a sound body.) *Recommends a healthy body for a sound mind.*

1123. **MESTIZO educado, diablo colorado.** (An educated mestizo turns into a red devil.) *A colonial opinion of an educated person of mixed blood.*

1124. **MIEL en la boca y guarda la bolsa.** (Honey in your mouth and save your money.) *Give lip service, keep your money.*

1125. **MIENTRAS al cielo no subas, nos veremos.** (As long as you don't go to heaven, we'll meet again.) *It's a small world.*

1126. **MIENTRAS DURA, vida y dulzura.** (While it lasts, a good life and great pleasure.) *Eat, drink, and be merry for tomorrow we die.*

1127. **MIENTRAS en mi casa estoy, rey soy.** (While I am in' my home, I am king.) *Every man's house is his castle.*

1128. **MIENTRAS HAY ALMA, hay esperanza.** (While there's a soul, there's hope.) *Where there's life, there's hope.*

1129. **MIENTRAS VIDA DURE, tiempo sobra.** (While there's life, time is abundant.) *Where there's life, there's hope.*

1130. **MIRA bien y con cuidado y en toda empresa determinado.** (Observe and look carefully and act with resolve in all enterprises.) *Be sure you're right, then proceed.*

1131. **MÍROTE A DESEO, hueles a poleo; mírote cada rato, hueles a chivato.** (Seeing you when I wish, you smell

of mint; seeing you too often, you smell like a goat.)
Familiarity breeds contempt.

1132. **MIROTE A OSCURAS y agárrote a tientas.** (I see you in the dark and grab you by groping.) *Said of a person who is eavesdropping.*

1133. **MISA de dos curas nunca es buena.** (A mass said by two priests is never good.) *Too many cooks spoil the broth.*

1134. **MUCHO AYUDA el que no estorba.** (He who isn't in the way is helpful.) *A sarcastic way of telling a person to get out of the way.*

1135. **MUCHO AYUNA el que mal come.** (He fasts much who eats little.) *Suggests that the poor should not be asked to make sacrifices, due to their financial straits.*

1136. **MUCHO HABLAR, mucho errar.** (He errs much who talks much.) *Much talk, no action.*

1137. **MUCHO RUIDO, poco trabajo.** (Much noise, little work.) *Much talk, no action.*

1138. **MUCHO RUIDO y pocas nueces.** (Much noise and few nuts.) *Great talkers are little doers.*

1139. **MUCHO SABE la zorra pero más el que la pesca.** (The fox is clever but he who catches her is more clever.) *Clever people always find their match.*

1140. **MUCHOS AMENES al cielo llegan.** (Many amens get to heaven.) *He who perseveres goes far.*

1141. **MUCHOS CABITOS hacen un cirio pascual.** (Many candle ends make a large candle.) *Penny and penny laid up will be many.*

1142. **MUCHOS CONOCIDOS pero pocos amigos.** (Many acquaintances but few friends.) *Recommends choosing our friends carefully.*

1143. **MUCHOS POCOS hacen un mucho.** (Many littles make a lot.) *Many a little makes a mickle.*

1144. **MUCHO VA de Pedro a Pedro.** (There is quite a difference between one Pete and another.) *No two men are alike.*

1145. **MUDA el lobo los dientes pero no las mientes.** (The wolf loses his teeth but not his ways.) *The leopard can't change his spots.*

1146. **MUERTE deseada, vida durada.** (He who longs for death lives longest.) *A comment on how people who always want to die seem to live forever.*

1147. **MUERTE no venga que achaque no tenga.** (Death doesn't come without an excuse.) *An ironic way of saying that people will always find excuses to get around doing some disagreeable task.*

1148. **MUJER de *tahure*, nunca te alegres, porque si hoy ganas, mañana pierdes.** (Oh, wife of a gambler, do not rejoice, for if you win today, tomorrow you lose.) *Life has its ups and downs.*

1149. **MUJER que no tiene tacha, chapalea 'l agua y no se moja.** (An honest woman can dabble in the water and not get wet.) *An honest woman can be surrounded by bad company and remain untainted.*

1150. **MURIO el perro y se acabó la rabia.** (When the dog died his rabies died.) *The beast dead, the venom dead.*

1151. **MUSICA pagada, hace mal son.** (Music paid for in advance sounds flat.) *Paying in advance for a job doesn't always get good results.*

1152. **MUSICA pagada, mal sonada.** (Music paid for in advance sounds bad.) *Paying for a job in advance doesn't always get good results.*

103

No des paso sin *huarache*.
Don't take a step without your sandals.

1153. **NADA le hace la lagaña al *huero*, antes le está cuando llora.** (Bleariness is not detracting in an Anglo; in fact, it compliments him when he cries.) *An opinion that almost anything looks well on an Anglo, while the same things are criticized on a Spanish-speaking person.*

1154. **NADA quita lo valiente a lo cortés.** (Being brave detracts nothing from being courteous.) *The brave should not think it beneath them to be courteous.*

1155. **NADAR, NADAR y a la orilla 'hogar.** (After swimming so hard one drowns upon reaching the shore.) *A complaint on losing, at the last moment, something that has taken a lifetime to achieve.*

1156. **NADIE diga—De esta agua no beberé.** (Let no one say, "I will not drink this water.") *Never say never.*

1157. **NADIE diga de sí nada, que sus obras lo dirán.** (Let no one say anything in his own favor, his deeds will say it.) *A man is known by his works.*

1158. **NADIE diga que es querido (aunque lo estén adorando).** (Let no one say he is loved, even though he is being adored.) *Don't count your chickens before they are hatched.*

1159. NADIE diga zape hasta que no escape. (Let no one say zape until he escapes.) *Don't whistle until you're out of the woods.*

1160. NADIE PUEDE servir a dos señores. (No one can serve two masters.) *No one can serve two masters.*

1161. NADIE SABE el bien que tiene hasta que lo ve perdido. (No one knows the fortune he has until he loses it.) *We never miss the sunshine until the shadows come.*

1162. NADIE SABE lo que hay en l' olla como el meneador que la menea. (No one knows what's in the pot better than the ladle that stirs it.) *Only one knows where the shoe pinches.*

1163. NADIE SABE para quién trabaja. (No one knows for whom he toils.) *One sows and another reaps.*

1164. NADIE SEA tuerto y nadie se lo dirá. (Let no one be one-eyed and no one will tell him he is.) *He who has defects will be criticized.*

1165. NATURAL y figura, hasta la sepultura. (Disposition and figure are with one from birth to the grave.) *What is bred in the bone will never come out of the flesh.*

1166. NI AL NIÑO el *bollo,* ni al santo el voto. (Don't promise a child a cookie or a saint a vow.) *Warns against empty promises.*

1167. NI FEA que espante, ni hermosa que encante. (Neither a woman that scares people nor one that enchants them.) *Neither too ugly nor too beautiful a wife.*

1168. NINGUN JOROBADO se ve la joroba. (No hunchback sees his hump.) *People are never aware of their shortcomings.*

1169. NINGUNO cante victoria aunque en el estribo esté. (Let no one sing victory even though he may be about to gain it.) *Don't count your chickens before they're hatched.*

1170. NINGUNO DIGA, De esta agua no beberé. (Let no one say, "Of this water I shall not drink.") *Never say never.*

1171. **NINGUNO DIGA quién es, que sus obras lo dirán.** (Let no one say who he is, for his works will say it.) *A man is known by his works.*

1172. **NINGUNO DIGA zape hasta que no escape.** (Let no one say zape until he escapes.) *Don't whistle until you're out of the woods.*

1173. **NIÑAS criadas con abueles, nunca buenas.** (Little girls raised by their grandmothers are never good.) *A belief that girls reared by their grandmothers are spoiled.*

1174. **NIÑO que no llora, no mama.** (The child that does not cry does not get fed.) *The wheel that squeaks gets the most grease.*

1175. **NI SABADO sin sol, ni fea sin amor.** (Neither a Saturday without sun, nor a homely girl without love.) *Suggests that everything occurs in a determined manner.*

1176. **NI TODO lo que sepas digas, ni todo lo que tengas da.** (Neither say everything you know, nor give everything you have.) *Moderation in all things.*

1177. **NI UN DEDO hace una mano, ni una golondrina un verano.** (One finger does not make a hand, or one swallow a summer.) *One exception does not make a rule.*

1178. **NI VEAS MAL todo lo viejo, ni alabes todo lo nuevo.** (Neither despise all the old nor praise all the new.) *Moderation in all things.*

1179. **NO ACARICIES el gato sin ponerte guantes.** (Don't pet the cat without putting on your gloves.) *An ounce of prevention is worth a pound of cure.*

1180. **NO ANDES antes de gatear; ni corras antes de andar.** (Do not walk before you crawl, or run before you walk.) *Preparation is the secret of success.*

1181. **¡NO A TODOS les pasa!** (It doesn't happen to everyone!) *An expression used to criticize a person for being awkward.*

1182. **NOCHE alegre, mañanita triste.** (A night of revelry, a morning of regret.) *A night of dissipation is followed by a morning of grief.*

1183. NO CON quien naces sino con quien paces. (Not with whom you are born but with whom you associate.) *A man is judged by the company he keeps.*

1184. NO CREAS todo lo que veas ni tampoco la mitad de lo que oigas. (Don't believe everything you see, or half of what you hear.) *Believe only what you see or hear yourself.*

1185. NO CUENTES las ganancias antes de empezar la obra. (Don't count your profits before starting the job.) *Don't count your chickens before they're hatched.*

1186. NO DA el que puede sino el que quiere. (Not one who can give but one who is willing to give.) *Where there's a will, there's a way.*

1187. NO DEJES camino por vereda. (Don't abandon the road for a path.) *Don't give up a sure thing for one that is uncertain.*

1188. NO DEJES para mañana lo que puedas hacer hoy. (Don't leave for tomorrow what you can do today.) *Don't put off for tomorrow what you can do today.*

1189. NO DES PASO sin *huarache*. (Don't take a step without your sandals.) *Look before you leap.*

1190. NO DES TU BRAZO a torcer. (Don't allow your arm to be twisted.) *Stand fast.*

1191. NO DICE más la lengua que lo que siente el corazón. (The tongue says no more than the heart feels.) *Out of the fullness of the heart the mouth speaks.*

1192. NO DONDE naces, sino donde paces. (Not where you were born but where you're making a living.) *Home is where you hang your hat.*

1193. NO ECHAMOS de menos el agua hasta que se seca la noria. (We never miss the water until the well dries up.) *We never miss the sunshine until the shadows come.*

1194. NO ES BORRACHO el que ha bebido sino el que sigue bebiendo. (He who drinks is not a drunkard, but he who continues is.) *He who drinks is not a drunkard, but he who keeps drinking is.*

1195. **NO ES BUENO el indio pero su *guayabe* sí.** (The Indian is no good but his bread certainly is.) *Censures those who discriminate against Indians, yet are ready to exploit them.*

1196. **NO ES CANTAR en el llano como arrimarse a la vihuela.** (It's one thing to sing in the plains and another to sing with guitar accompaniment.) *Saying and doing are two different things.*

1197. **NO ES COSA del otro jueves.** (It isn't anything that happened last Thursday.) *Said of something that seldom occurs.*

1198. **NO ES CULPA del gallo sino del amarrador.** (The rooster is not to blame, but rather he who got him ready.) *Said to someone who finds a ready excuse for something he did wrong.*

1199. **NO ES DECIRLAS como comerlas.** (It isn't the same to say it as to eat it.) *Criticizing something and being able to do it are two different things.*

1200. **NO ES EL LEON como lo pintan.** (The lion is not as he is painted.) *His bark is worse than his bite.*

1201. **NO ES LO MISMO hablar de toros que estar en el redondel.** (It is not the same to discuss bulls as it is to be in the bullring.) *Criticizing a performance and doing it yourself are two different things.*

1202. **NO ES LO MISMO VER comer que tirarse con los platos.** (Seeing someone eat and throwing the dishes at each other are two different things.) *Criticizing a performance and doing it yourself are two different things.*

1203. **NO ES ORO todo lo que reluce.** (All that glitters is not gold.) *Appearances are deceiving.*

1204. **NO ES TAN FEO el león como lo pintan.** (The lion is not as ugly as he is painted.) *People tend to exaggerate things and make a mountain out of a molehill.*

1205. **NO ES TANTO la meada como la pasada del colchón.** (Wetting the bed is not so bad; soaking the mattress is

108

what's sad.) *Suggests that the consequences of an act can be worse than the act itself.*

1206. **NO ES TARDE el bien, como venga.** (Good fortune is never late as long as it comes.) *Better late than never.*

1207. **NO ES VERLAS como experimentarlas.** (It's not the same to observe something as to experience it.) *Seeing is one thing; experiencing is another.*

1208. **NO FALTA un roto para un descosido.** (There will always be a ragged person for another who's tattered.) *Every Jack has his Jill.*

1209. **NO FIRMES carta que no leas, ni bebas agua que no veas.** (Don't sign anything without reading it or drink water that you cannot see.) *Advises one to be careful of what one signs.*

1210. **NO HAGAS cosas buenas que a la vista parezcan malas.** (Don't do anything good that gives the appearance of being bad.) *Implies that people judge others by appearances.*

1211. **NO HAGAS lo que no puedas, ni gastes lo que no tengas.** (Don't do what you cannot, or spend what you do not have.) *Advises against being a spendthrift.*

1212. **NO HAGAS MAL que bien no esperes.** (Don't do wrong if you expect kindness.) *Do unto others as you would have them do unto you.*

1213. **NO HALLARAS un avariento que esté tranquilo y contento.** (You will not find a miser that is calm and contented.) *A comment on the unhappiness of misers.*

1214. **NO HAY AMOR como el primero.** (There is no love like the first.) *There's no love like one's first love.*

1215. **NO HAY AMOR sin interés.** (No love without interest.) *There's no love without self interest.*

1216. **NO HAY A QUIEN no le guste un caldito de cebolla.** (There is no one that doesn't like a little onion soup.) *Everyone enjoys a little flattery now and then.*

1217. **NO HAY ATAJO sin trabajo.** (There's no shortcut without work.) *The longest way around is the shortest way home.*

1218. NO HAY BODA sin tornaboda. (There is no marriage without its day after.) *There is no good time without the corresponding bad time.*

1219. NO HAY BONITA sin pero, ni fea sin gracia. (There is neither a pretty girl without some flaw nor an ugly one without some charm.) *Suggests the use of common sense in choosing a future wife.*

1220. NO HAY BORRACHO que coma lumbre. (There's not a drunkard that will eat fire.) *No one in his right mind will do things that will harm him.*

1221. NO HAY COMO lo propio porque lo ajeno no es verdad. (There's nothing like one's own things, for the other fellow's are not true.) *A recommendation that one appreciate one's own things.*

1222. NO HAY CORAZON MAS NEGRO que el que no sabe agradecer. (There's no heart so black as one that's unappreciative.) *No heart so black as an ungrateful one.*

1223. NO HAY CORAZON que a su dueño engañe. (There's no heart that will fool its master.) *You can fool others, but you cannot fool yourself.*

1224. NO HAY CORAZON TAN TRISTE como una bolsa sin dinero. (There's no heart so sad as a pocket without money.) *Money is happiness to him who needs it.*

1225. NO HAY COSA MALA que para algo no valga. (There's no bad thing that won't be of value to someone.) *All things have some value.*

1226. NO HAY COSA MAS BARATA que la que se compra. (There is nothing so cheap as that which is bought.) *Things we buy ourselves have no strings attached.*

1227. NO HAY COSAS MAS BARATAS que las buenas palabras. (There's nothing so cheap as kind words.) *Giving compliments never hurt anyone.*

1228. NO HAY cuña peor como la del mismo palo. (No

wedge is so strong as that which comes from the same wood.) *One's relatives can hurt us worse than the worst enemy.*

1229. **NO HAY DOLOR que al alma llegue que a los tres días no se quite.** (There's no pain which reaches the soul that will not go away by the third day.) *Time cures all pain.*

1230. **NO HAY HATAJO sin trabajo.** (There's no flock without toil.) *No gains without pains.*

1231. **NO HAY LIBRO tan malo que no tenga algo bueno.** (There is no book so bad that it has no good in it.) *There's good in all things.*

1232. **NO HAY LOCO que coma lumbre.** (There is no madman that will eat fire.) *No one in his right mind will do anything that will harm him.*

1233. **NO HAY MAL que cien años dure.** (There is no illness that will last a hundred years.) *Every cloud has a silver lining.*

1234. **NO HAY MAL que por bien no venga.** (There's no ill that brings no benefit.) *It's an ill wind that blows nobody good.*

1235. **NO HAY MAS AMIGO que Dios ni más pariente que un peso.** (There's no greater friend than God or closer relative than a dollar.) *God and money in one's pocket are the greatest friends.*

1236. **NO HAY más que un octubre en el año.** (There is only one October in the year.) *Opportunity knocks but once.*

1237. **NO HAY MAYOR MAL que el descontento de cada cual.** (There's no worse evil than each one's discontentment.) *Dissatisfaction is the worst of evils.*

1238. **NO HAY MEJOR AMANSADOR que el *casorio*.** (There's no better tamer than marriage.) *Marriage settles a person.*

1239. **NO HAY MEJOR BOCADO que el robado.** (There's no better morsel than a stolen one.) *Forbidden fruit is the sweetest.*

111

1240. NO HAY MEJOR COLCHON que un buen sueño.
(There's no better mattress than being really sleepy.)
If one is really sleepy he won't mind a bad mattress.

1241. NO HAY MEJOR ESCUELA que la que el tiempo da.
(There's no better school than that which time gives.)
Experience is the best teacher.

1242. NO HAY MEJOR ESPEJO que el amigo. (There's no
better mirror than one's friend.) *A true friend will tell
you how you really look.*

1243. NO HAY MEJOR SALSA que un buen apetito. (There's
no better sauce than a hearty appetite.) *Hunger is the
best sauce.*

1244. NO HAY NADA FUERTE para la muerte. (There's
nothing too strong for death.) *There's no escaping
death.*

1245. NO HAY PEOR CIEGO que el que no quiere ver.
(There's no worse blind man than he who refuses to
see.) *Comments on the stubbornness of some people.*

1246. NO HAY PEOR CUÑA que la del mismo palo. (There's
no worse wedge than that which comes from the same
wood.) *There's no worse enemy than a relative or
friend alienated.*

1247. NO HAY PEOR LUCHA que la que no se hace. (There's
no worse effort than that which is never made.) *Nothing
ventured, nothing gained.*

1248. NO HAY PEOR SORDO que el que no quiere oír.
(There's no worse deaf man than he who will not listen.) *Comments on the stubbornness of people who
refuse to listen to others.*

1249. NO HAY QUE MENTAR la soga en casa del 'horcado.
(One should not mention rope in the home of one that
has been hanged.) *Recommends being careful not to
hurt people's feelings on subjects that may be embar-
rassing to them.*

1250. NO HAY QUE PREDICAR vigilia y comer carne. (One
should not preach vigil and eat meat.) *Practice what
you preach.*

1251. **NO HAY QUINCE años feos.** (There's no fifteen-year-old that is homely.) *At fifteen all have some charm or attraction.*

1252. **NO HAY REGLA sin excepción.** (There's no rule without its exception.) *There are exceptions to every rule.*

1253. **NO HAY ROSA sin espina.** (There's no rose without a thorn.) *No gains without pains.*

1254. **NO HAY SABADO sin sol ni domingo sin ranchero.** (There's no Saturday without sun, nor Sunday without a rancher.) *Said of an event or happening that occurs without fail.*

1255. **NO HAY VIDA más cansada que el eterno no hacer nada.** (There's no life so boring as not having anything to do.) *No life so boring as a life of idleness.*

1256. **NO LE BUSQUES tres pies al gato.** (Don't look for three legs on the cat.) *Don't look for trouble lest you find it.*

1257. **NO LE HACE que nazcan ciegos, ellos pedirán limosna.** (It doesn't matter if they are born blind, they will ask for alms.) *Suggests the inevitable.*

1258. **NO LLORES la nieve antes que caiga.** (Don't cry because its snowing before it falls.) *Don't complain before calamity strikes.*

1259. **NO LO HAGAS, no lo temas.** (Don't do it and don't fear it.) *Do no evil and fear no evil.*

1260. **NO LO HAGAS y no lo dirán.** (Don't do it and no one will say anything.) *Suggests not doing anything that will expose one to criticism.*

1261. **NO LO QUE FUISTE, sino lo que eres.** (Not what you were but what you are.) *Our lineage begins with ourselves.*

1262. **NOMAS cuando hay relámpagos se acuerdan de Santa Bárbara.** (Only when there's lightning does one remember St. Barbara.) *People forget God until there's a dire necessity.*

1263. **NOMAS cuando relampaguea se acuerdan de Santa Bárbara.** (Only when it's lightning does one remem-

113

ber St. Barbara.) *People forget God 'till there's a dire necessity.*

1264. **NOMAS cuando truena se acuerdan de Santa Bárbara.** (They think of St. Barbara only when there is thunder.) *People forget God 'till there's a dire necessity.*

1265. **NOMAS el que carga el saco sabe lo que lleva dentro.** (Only he who is carrying the bag knows what it contains.) *Only he who wears the shoe knows where it pinches.*

1266. **NO ME DEFIENDAS, compadre.** (Don't defend me, old friend.) *With friends like you, who needs enemies?*

1267. **NO ME DIGAN tío, porque ni parientes somos.** (Don't call me uncle, we're not even related.) *Said when a person shuns unwanted companions.*

1268. **NO ME RAJEN tanta leña que ya no tengo fogón.** (Don't split so much wood for me, I no longer have a furnace.) *Closing the barn door after the horse is stolen.*

1269. **NO NECESITO** *aretes,* **y por eso no los uso.** (I don't need earrings, and that's why I don't wear them.) *Said when children want to tag along though we don't want them to do so.*

1270. **NO POR mucho madrugar amanece más temprano.** (Getting up very early doesn't make it dawn any sooner.) *Suggests that one cannot rush the natural course of things.*

1271. **NOS CAYO la** *sopa* **en la miel.** (Our bread pudding fell right into our honey.) *Said when people get a windfall.*

1272. **NO SE ACUERDA EL CURA de cuando era sacristán.** (The priest doesn't remember he was once a sexton.) *Those who rise in the world are apt to forget their beginnings.*

1273. **NO SE ACUERDA LA SUEGRA que fue nuera.** (The mother-in-law doesn't remember she was once a daughter-in-law.) *People who rise in their profession often forget what subordinates are going through.*

1274. **NO SE APURE pa que dure.** (Don't hurry, so you will

114

last long.) *Advises us to take life as it comes and not worry unduly.*

1275. **NO SE ganó Zamora en una hora.** (Zamora wasn't conquered in a day.) *Rome wasn't built in a day.*

1276. **NO SE HACE blanca la que es trigueña aunque la laven con agua de la peña.** (No amount of scrubbing can make a blonde out of a brunette.) *Suggests that one cannot change one's appearance.*

1277. **NO SE HIZO la miel para la boca del burro.** (Honey was not meant for the mouth of the donkey.) *Cast no pearls before swine.*

1278. **NO SE PUEDE CARGAR el muerto y cantar el alabado.** (You can't carry the corpse and sing the *alabado*.) *You can't do two different things at the same time.*

1279. **NO SE PUEDE CHIFLAR y comer pinole.** (You can't whistle and eat *pinole*.) *You can't do two different things at the same time.*

1280. **NO SE PUEDE REPICAR y en la procesión estar.** (You can't ring the church bell and take part in the procession.) *You can't do two different things at the same time.*

1281. **NO SE VE LA COLA la zorra pero sí la ajena.** (The fox can't see his tail but he does see the other fox's.) *We often see other people's faults but very seldom our own.*

1282. **NO TE VAYAS al color que también la vista engaña.** (Don't go by the color, for the eye can also deceive.) *Don't judge a book by its cover.*

1283. **NO TIENE LA CULPA el indio sino el que lo hace compadre.** (The Indian is not to blame, but rather he who befriends him.) *Said when we complain of getting cheated by someone we should not have trusted in the first place.*

1284. **NO TODA LA GALLINA que cacarea pone huevo.** (Not every hen that cackles lays an egg.) *Great talkers are little doers.*

1285. **NO TODO EL QUE TRAE LEVITA, es persona *prencipal.*** (Not everyone who wears a jacket is important.) *Don't judge a book by its cover.*

1286. **NO TODO LO BLANCO es harina.** (Not everything white is flour.) *All that glitters is not gold.*

1287. **NO TODO LO DE BUEN AROMA es perfume.** (Not everything with a pleasant scent is perfume.) *All that glitters is not gold.*

1288. **NO TODO LO QUE RELUMBRA es oro.** (Not everything that shines is gold.) *All that glitters is not gold.*

1289. **NO TODO LO QUE TIENE PELO es cepillo.** (Not everything with hair is a brush.) *All that glitters is not gold.*

1290. **NO TODOS los días se muere un burro.** (A donkey doesn't die every day.) *Fortune is fickle.*

1291. **NO TODOS los que chiflan son arrieros.** (Not everyone that whistles is a muleteer.) *Knowing something about a job does not make one an expert.*

1292. **NUNCA DEJES para mañana lo que puedas hacer hoy.** (Never leave for tomorrow what you can do today.) *Don't leave for tomorrow what you can do today.*

1293. **NUNCA FUE PRIOR Fray Modesto.** (Friar Modestus never became prior.) *Faint heart never won fair lady.*

1294. **NUNCA LLUEVE a gusto de todos.** (It never rains to everyone's satisfaction.) *You can't please everybody.*

Oración de perro no va al cielo.
A dog's prayer does not get to heaven.

1295. **OBRA EMPEZADA, medio acabada.** (A work begun is half done.) *Well begun is half done.*

1296. **OBRAS SON AMORES, no razones.** (Actions spell love, not words.) *Actions speak louder than words.*

1297. **OFRECER sí, pero dar no.** (Offer, yes, but give, no.) *Recommends that one not squander his possessions.*

1298. **OIR CANTAR el gallo y no saber dónde.** (To hear the rooster crow and not know where.) *To talk through one's hat.*

1299. **OIR, ver y callar.** (Hear, look, and keep silent.) *Mind your own business.*

1300. **OJO no engaña.** (The eye does not deceive.) *Seeing is believing.*

1301. **OJO PENDIENTE no miente.** (An alert eye does not lie.) *Suggests that one keep his eyes open to know what's going on.*

1302. **OJO POR OJO y diente por diente.** (Eye for eye and tooth for tooth.) *An eye for an eye and a tooth for a tooth.*

1303. **OJO QUE NO MIRA no antoja.** (An eye that does not

see does not desire.) *Take away the temptation and avoid the sin.*

1304. **OJOS CERRADOS no indican ceguera.** (Closed eyes do not indicate blindness.) *Don't be misled by appearances.*

1305. **OJOS QUE NO VEN, corazón que no siente.** (Eyes that don't see, heart that won't feel.) *Out of sight, out of mind.*

1306. **OJOS QUE NO VEN tienen menos que sentir.** (Eyes that do not see have less to feel.) *Out of sight, out of mind.*

1307. **¡OJOS que te vieron ir!** (Oh, eyes that saw you leave!) *An opportunity lost never returns.*

1308. **OJOS VEMOS, corazón no sabemos.** (Eyes we see, heart we know not.) *It's hard to tell what people have in their hearts.*

1309. **OLLA que mucho *jierve* sabor pierde.** (A pot that boils too long loses its flavor.) *Familiarity breeds contempt.*

1310. **OLVIDAR la injuria es la mejor venganza.** (To forget the injustice is the best revenge.) *The noblest part of vengeance is to forget the offense.*

1311. **ORACION de perro no va al cielo.** (A dog's prayer does not get to heaven.) *An unreasonable request is seldom granted.*

1312. **ORO es lo que oro vale.** (Gold is what gold is worth.) *The value of gold lies in its buying power.*

1313. **O TODOS HIJOS o todos entenados.** (Either we're all children or we're all stepchildren.) *Said when people demand to be treated equally.*

1314. **¡OTRA VEZ LA BURRA al trigo y por la misma veredita!** (The donkey's in the wheat again and took the same little path!) *Here we go again!*

1315. **¡OTRO VEZ LA BURRA al trigo y el burrito al *alberjón!*** (The donkey's in the wheat again and the little donkey is in the peas!) *Here we go again!*

118

1316. OVEJA CHIQUITA cada año es corderita. (A small sheep looks like a lamb year in and year out.) *Persons of small stature hide their age well.*

1317. OVEJA QUE BALA, bocado pierde. (The sheep that bleats loses his mouthful.) *Recommends not letting anything distract us from our purpose.*

Para prosperar, madrugar.
In order to prosper, get up early.

1318. **PACIENCIA y barajar.** (Be patient and keep shuffling the cards.) *If at first you don't succeed, try, try again.*

1319. **PAGA lo que debes, sabrás lo que tienes.** (Pay off what you owe and you'll know what you have.) *We never know what we actually have until we liquidate our bills.*

1320. **PALABRA y piedra suelta no tienen vuelta.** (Loose words and stones have no return.) *Foolish words, like flying stones, cannot be called back.*

1321. **PALABRAS y plumas se las lleva el viento.** (Words and feathers are carried away by the wind.) *Actions speak louder than words.*

1322. **PAL ENFERMO que es de vida, 'l agua le es medicina.** (The patient who is to live will get well with water.) *A strong constitution is one's best medicine.*

1323. **PALO dado ni Dios lo quita.** (Once a blow is struck, not even God can take it away.) *What's done cannot be undone.*

1324. **PAL SANTO que es la misa, con un repique basta.** (Considering the importance of the saint, one ring's enough.) *People should be treated according to their importance.*

1325. **PAN CALIENTE, fuera diente.** (Hot bread, goodbye teeth.) *A belief that eating hot bread is not good for one's health.*

1326. **PAN COMIDO, compañía deshecha.** (The bread eaten, the company dispersed.) *Censures those who desert us, once we are no longer needed.*

1327. **PAN COMIENDO y 'cemitas repartiendo.** (Eating bread and distributing wholewheat bread.) *He who distributes often keeps the best part for himself.*

1328. **PAN DURO, pero seguro.** (Stale bread but bread for sure.) *Half a loaf is better than none.*

1329. **PAN PARA HOY y hambre para mañana.** (Bread today and hunger tomorrow.) *Said of unreliable people or things.*

1330. **PAN SIN SAL y duro es mejor que ninguno.** (Stale or unsalted bread is better than none.) *Half a loaf is better than none.*

1331. **PANZA llena, corazón contento.** (A full belly, a happy heart.) *Happiness is a full stomach.*

1332. **PAPAS frías en mi casa son mejores que carne asada en la del vecino.** (Cold potatoes at home taste better than roast at the neighbors.) *Be it ever so humble, there's no place like home.*

1333. **PARA BUEN PERRO, buen amo.** (For a good dog, a good master.) *Workmen perform better when they are treated well.*

1334. **PARA CADA PERRO hay su garrote.** (Every dog has his cudgel.) *Every problem has its solution.*

1335. **PARA DAR CONSEJOS, todos; para tomarlos, pocos.** (To give advice, all; to take it, few.) *Everyone is ready to give advice, but few are ready to take it.*

1336. **PARA DECIR MENTIRAS y comer pescado, se necesita mucho cuidado.** (When telling lies and eating fish, one should take great care.) *A liar is soon found out.*

1337. **PARA DONDE VA LA GENTE, va Clemente.** (Where the people go, Clement goes.) *Monkey see, monkey do.*

1338. **PARA EL AMOR no hay fronteras.** (In love there are no frontiers.) *Love knows no bounds.*

1339. **PARA EL BURRO, la ceniza es delicia.** (Ashes are a joy to donkeys.) *People love things or habits they are used to.*

1340. **PARA EL SANTO que es la misa, con un repique basta.** (Considering the saint, one ring is sufficient.) *People are treated according to their importance.*

1341. **PARA LOS ARREPENTIDOS es el reino de los cielos.** (For the repentant is the kingdom of heaven.) *The kingdom of heaven is for those who repent.*

1342. **PARA MAÑANA, las cosas de mañana; para hoy las de hoy.** (Leave tomorrow's things for tomorrow and do the things that should be done today.) *First things first.*

1343. **PARA MORIRSE de hambre, con no comer basta.** (To die from hunger one only needs to forgo food.) *A sarcastic remark said when people don't put enough food on the table.*

1344. **PARA PENDEJO no se necesita maestro.** (To be a fool needs no school.) *Refers to making a mistake that could easily have been avoided.*

1345. **PARA PROSPERAR, madrugar.** (In order to prosper, get up early.) *The early bird catches the worm.*

1346. **¿PARA QUE PEDIRLE a los santos, habiendo tan lindo Dios?** (Why pray to the saints when we can pray to God?) *Suggests not going to subordinates but directly to the boss.*

1347. **PARA QUIEN es mi *nana,* bueno está mi *tata.*** (Considering who my mother is, my father is good enough for her.) *A sarcastic remark for those who think they are above us.*

1348. **PARA TODO HAY REMEDIO, menos para la muerte.** (There's a cure for everything except death.) *All problems have a solution.*

1349. **PARA TODO MAL, mezcal; para todo bien, tambíen.**

(Mescal is good for joy and sadness.) *An expression used by those who need an excuse for drinking.*

1350. **PARA TONTO no se estudia.** (One needs no school to be a fool.) *Said to persons who make silly mistakes.*

1351. **PARA UN BUEN HAMBRE no hay pan duro.** (There's no stale bread when one is really hungry.) *Hunger is the best sauce.*

1352. **PARA UN MADRUGADOR, otro que no duerme.** (For an early riser, one who never sleeps.) *However good you may think you are, there will always be someone better than you.*

1353. **PARIENTES Y EL SOL, entre más lejos, mejor.** (Relatives and the sun, the farther away, the better.) *Relatives and people who annoy us are better at a distance.*

1354. **PARIENTES y *trastes* viejos, pocos y lejos.** (Relatives and old dishes, few and far away. *Relatives and people who annoy us are better at a distance.*

1355. **PASADO el tranco, olvidado el santo.** (The distance covered, the saint forgotten.) *The danger past, the saint forgotten.*

1356. **PASO a paso se cubre buen pedazo.** (Step by step, one covers a lot of ground.) *He who perseveres goes far.*

1357. **PEDIR limosna para hacer caridad.** (To beg in order to do charity work.) *Robbing Peter to pay Paul.*

1358. **PEDRO GOMEZ, tú lo traes y tú lo comes.** (Peter Gomez, you bring it and you eat it.) *Said of people who bring home some delicacy and eat more than the family for whom they brought the food.*

1359. **PEDRO la hace y Juan la paga.** (Peter does it and John pays for it.) *To get blamed for something someone else did.*

1360. **PEDRO PINO fue y Pedro Pino vino.** (Pedro Pino left and Pedro Pino he returned.) *Said of people who go out to accomplish a thing and return just as they left, that is, without accomplishing anything.*

123

1361. PERDONAR AL MALO es dejarlo que lo sea. (Forgiving an evil person is to let him be evil.) *Suggests punishment for evildoers.*

1362. PERDONAR MEJOR que vengar. (To pardon is better than to avenge.) *Better to pardon than to avenge.*

1363. PERRO LADRADOR, poco mordedor. (A barking dog rarely ever bites.) *His bark is worse than his bite.*

1364. PERRO QUE DA en comer huevos, aunque le quemen el hocico. (The dog that starts eating eggs will do it even if you burn his snout.) *Bad habits are hard to break.*

1365. PERRO QUE LADRA no muerde. (A barking dog never bites.) *His bark is worse than his bite.*

1366. PERRO QUE NO SALE no encuentra hueso. (The dog that doesn't go out doesn't find a bone.) *Said to people who'd rather stay home than go out to look for a job.*

1367. PERSONA prevenida nunca fue vencida. (The person who is prepared is never vanquished.) *Forewarned is forearmed.*

1368. PIEDRA movediza el musgo no la cobija. (A moving rock allows no moss.) *A rolling stone gathers no moss.*

1369. PIEDRA movediza no cría *enlame*. (A moving rock allows no slime.) *A rolling stone gathers no moss.*

1370. PIEDRA movediza no cría *mojo*. (A moving rock allows no rust.) *A rolling stone gathers no moss.*

1371. PIEDRA movediza nunca *mojo* la cobija. (A moving rock never gets rusty.) *A rolling stone gathers no moss.*

1372. PIEDRA que rueda no cría *mojo*. (A rock that rolls doesn't get rusty.) *A rolling stone gathers no moss.*

1373. PIENSA el ladrón que todos son de su condición. (The thief thinks that everyone is like he is.) *The thief thinks that everyone is a thief.*

1374. PIENSAN los enamorados que todos andan con los

ojos vendados. (Lovers think everyone is blindfolded.) *Love is blind.*

1375. **PINO fue y Pino vino.** (Mr. Pino departed and Mr. Pino returned.) *Said of people who start out to accomplish something and return empty-handed.*

1376. **PLATO ajeno, parece más lleno.** (The other fellow's plate seems fuller.) *The grass always looks greener on the other side of the fence.*

1377. **PLEITOS con todos, menos con la cocinera.** (Fight everyone, except the cook.) *Warns against quarreling with those on whom we depend for a job, a living, etc.*

1378. **PLEITOS de enamorados, presto son olvidados.** (Lovers' quarrels are soon past.) *Lovers' quarrels are soon forgotten.*

1379. **¡POBRECITOS de los feos si no hubiera malos gustos!** (Pity the ugly if people didn't have bad taste!) *There is no accounting for tastes.*

1380. **POBRE con puro, ladrón seguro.** (A poor man with a cigar, certainly a thief.) *A poor man smoking a cigar is a thief for sure.*

1381. **POCO a poco se anda lejos.** (Little by little one goes far.) *Perseverance wins the race.*

1382. **POCO a poco se le saca 'l agua al coco.** (Little by little the coconut yields its water.) *He who perseveres goes far.*

1383. **POCO VENENO no mata pero ataranta.** (A little poison won't kill but it does make you dizzy.) *Used as an excuse by those who will accept a small amount of food or drink even while on a diet.*

1384. **POQUITO, porque es bendito.** (Just a little, because it is blessed.) *Said as an excuse for not giving an excessive amount of food or drink to someone.*

1385. **POR DINERO baila el perro.** (The dog will dance for money.) *Money talks.*

1386. **POR DONDE brinca la cabra brinca el cabrito.** (Wherever the goat jumps, the kid follows.) *Like father, like son.*

1387. **POR EL TEMPLO del trabajo se entra al de la fama.** (Through the temple of toil one enters the temple of fame.) *It takes hard work to attain one's dreams.*

1388. **POR LA BOCA muere el pez.** (Through its mouth, the fish dies.) *People who talk too much often give themselves away or put their foot in it.*

1389. **POR LAS ACCIONES se juzgan los corazones.** (Hearts are judged by people's actions.) *One's actions show his feelings.*

1390. **POR LAS VISPERAS se sacan los días.** (By the eve we get to know about the day.) *Certain signs tell us what results to expect.*

1391. **POR MUCHO MADRUGAR no amanece más temprano.** (Getting up early does not bring the dawn any sooner.) *Many times, despite our plans, we fail to attain our ends.*

1392. **POR TODAS PARTES se va a Roma.** (All roads lead to Rome.) *All means are good that will help us attain a good end.*

1393. **POR UN BORREGO no se juzga la manada.** (You can't judge the flock by one sheep.) *An entire group cannot be judged by one of its members.*

1394. **POR UN CENTAVO no se completa un peso.** (For lack of a penny you can't complete a dollar.) *Suggests that any amount of money, however small, is very important.*

1395. **POR UNO QUE SALGA CHUECO no todos están torcidos.** (One's turning out twisted doesn't mean that all are crooked.) *Don't judge a group by one of its members.*

1396. **POR VER la casa arder le prenden fuego a la mía.** (To see the house burn they set fire to mine.) *Censures those people who will go to any lengths to harm others.*

1397. **PREDICAS, pero no aplicas.** (You preach, but do not practice.) *Practice what you preach.*

1398. **PREGUNTA más el tonto en una hora de lo que contestan cien hombres en cien años.** (A fool can ask more questions in one hour than a hundred men can answer in a hundred years.) *It's easier to ask questions than to give answers.*

1399. **PREGUNTANDO se llega a Roma.** (By asking one's way one gets to Rome.) *Questioning and investigation will get us what we want to learn.*

1400. **PRESTA DINERO a un enemigo y lo ganarás; préstaselo a un amigo y lo perderás.** (Lend money to an enemy and you will win him over; lend it to a friend and you will lose him.) *Advice on lending money to friends.*

1401. **PRETENCIOSO, flojo y vano, mexicano.** (Pretentious, lazy and vain, Mexican.) *A poor opinion that some Mexicans have about themselves.*

1402. **PRIMERA ESPOSA, matrimonio, la segunda, compañía; la tercera, tontería.** (First wife, matrimony; second wife, company; the third—foolishness.) *Censures more than one marriage.*

1403. **PRIMERO ES COMER que ser cristiano.** (Eating comes before being a Christian.) *One's own personal needs should be attended to first.*

1404. **PRIMERO ES LA AMISTAD que el dinero.** (Friendship before money.) *Friendship is more valuable than money.*

1405. **PRIMERO LA OBLIGACION que la devoción.** (Obligation comes before devotion.) *Business before pleasure.*

1406. **PRIMERO MIS DIENTES que mis parientes.** (My teeth come before my relatives.) *One's own needs should receive one's attention first of all.*

1407. **PRIMERO MUERTO que rajado.** (I'd rather be dead than split.) *Preference for valor rather than cowardice.*

1408. **PRIMERO SOPITAS de miel y luego de hiel.** (First

comes the honey, then the bile.) *Things may turn out differently than they appear at first.*

1409. **PUEBLO chico, infierno grande.** (Small town, large hell.) *Living in a small town is bad, because everyone knows everyone else's business.*

1410. **PUEDE más el cuero que la camisa.** (The skin is stronger than the shirt.) *Blood is thicker than water.*

1411. **PUERTA abierta al justo tienta.** (An open door tempts the just.) *Take away the temptation and avoid the sin.*

Quien bien siembra, bien recoge.
As you sow, so shall you reap.

1412. QUE CORRAN a la *pilmama,* que ya el niño se divierte. (Get rid of the old baby-sitter, for the child is already amusing himself.) *A humorous expression used to point out an adult that is acting like a child.*

1413. ¿QUE CULPA tienen los indios que se alcen los navajoses? (Why should the Indians be blamed for the Navajos' uprising?) *One should not be blamed for another's woes.*

1414. ¿QUE CULPA tiene San Pedro que San Pablo esté pelón? (Why should St. Peter be blamed because St. Paul is bald?) *One should not be blamed for another's condition.*

1415. ¡QUE DIGAN MISA, si hay quien se la oiga! (Let them say Mass if there's anyone that will listen to it.) *An expression used to indicate that one doesn't care what others are saying about him.*

1416. ¿QUE FUERA DE LAS FEAS si no hubiera malos gustos? (What would become of the ugly if there were no poor tastes?) *There's no accounting for tastes.*

1417. ¿QUE HA DE DAR el encino sino bellotas? (What does the oak tree produce if not acorns?) *Uncouth people can only be expected to act rudely.*

1418. **¡QUE LE HACE la lagaña al *güero* hasta le está bien cuando llora!** (Bleariness in the eye of the blond is not detracting; in fact, it is becoming to him when he cries!) *Defects are little noticed in the virtuous.*

1419. **QUE QUIERE decirle el cántaro a la olla!** (What can` the pitcher say to the pot!) *The pot calling the kettle black.*

1420. **QUERER es poder.** (Desire is power.) *Where there's a will, there's a way.*

1421. **QUERER y aborrecer no puede a un tiempo ser.** (Loving and hating cannot happen at the same time.) *You can't do two different things at the same time.*

1422. **¡QUE SABE el burro de freno!** (What does the ass know about a bridle!) *You can't make a silk purse out of a sow's ear.*

1423. **¡QUE SE PIERDA y me haga daño, mejor que me haga daño!** (Between the food and making me ill, let it make me ill!) *Said when one eats leftovers rather than letting them go to waste.*

1424. **¡QUE SUSTO llevaron las gallinas!** (How frightened the chickens were!) *Said with a sigh of relief when one has been frightened.*

1425. **¡QUE TE IMPORTA, come torta de la mazorca!** (It's none of your business, stupid!) *Said to someone who asks something that is none of his business.*

1426. **¿QUE TIENE más el lechero que el que vende *jocoque?*** (What does the milkman have that the seller of buttermilk does not have?) *When two persons have equal rank and social standing, neither has reason to believe he is better than the other.*

1427. **¡QUE VIDA para sufrir en este mundo!** (What a life to suffer in this world!) *An exclamation used by those who show disgust for the state of things.*

1428. **QUIEN A BUEN ARBOL se arrima, buena sombra lo cobija.** (He who gets under a good tree finds good shade.) *A man is well off if he has friends or good connections.*

130

1429. **QUIEN ADELANTE no mira, atrás se queda.** (He who doesn't look ahead remains behind.) *Recommends being foresighted.*

1430. **QUIEN A FEA AMA, hermosa le parece.** (He who loves an ugly woman thinks her beautiful.) *Beauty is in the eye of the beholder.*

1431. **QUIEN ANDA CON CASADA tiene la vida prestada.** (He who goes with a married woman is living on borrowed time.) *A warning against going with a married woman.*

1432. **QUIEN A TU CASA no va, de la suya te destierra.** (He who does not go to your home banishes you from his.) *Said to people who do not visit you, as an excuse for not visiting them.*

1433. **QUIEN BIEN AMA nunca olvida.** (He who truly loves never forgets.) *A true love never forgets.*

1434. **QUIEN BIEN BAILA, de boda en boda anda.** (A good dancer goes from wedding dance to wedding dance.) *He who knows some art is welcome anywhere.*

1435. **QUIEN BIEN QUIERE a Beltrán, quiere a su can.** (He who really likes Beltran loves his dog.) *Love me, love my dog.*

1436. **QUIEN BIEN SIEMBRA, bien recoge.** (He who sows well, gathers well.) *As you sow, so shall you reap.*

1437. **QUIEN BIEN TE QUIERE te hará llorar.** (He who loves you will make you cry.) *A true friend will reprove and not flatter.*

1438. **QUIEN BUSCA, halla.** (He who seeks finds.) *Seek and you shall find.*

1439. **QUIEN CALLA, otorga.** (He who keeps silent consents.) *Silence gives consent.*

1440. **QUIEN CANTA, sus males espanta.** (He who sings drives away his worries.) *Sing your cares away.*

1441. **QUIEN COME la carne que ruña el hueso.** (He who eats the meat must gnaw the bone.) *No rose without a thorn.*

1442. **QUIEN COME PARA VIVIR, se alimenta; quien vive para comer, revienta.** (He who eats to live nourishes himself; he who lives to eat will burst.) *Eat to live, don't live to eat.*

1443. **QUIEN DA PAN a perro ajeno, pierde el pan y pierde el perro.** (He who gives bread to someone else's dog loses both his bread and the dog.) *People are ungrateful and do not always appreciate what we do for them.*

1444. **QUIEN DE ALACRAN está picado, la sombra lo espanta.** (He who has been bitten by a scorpion is easily frightened by its shadow.) *A burnt child dreads the fire.*

1445. **QUIEN DE LOS SUYOS se aleja, Dios lo deja.** (He who parts company with his family is forsaken by God.) *God forgets him who forsakes his people.*

1446. **QUIEN DUERME MUCHO, poco aprende.** (He who sleeps a great deal learns very little.) *One must be alert to be able to learn.*

1447. **QUIEN EVITA la ocasión, evita el ladrón.** (He who takes away the opportunity takes away the thief.) *He who guards against theft rarely meets a thief.*

1448. **¿QUIEN HA de comer 'cemita habiendo pan?** (Who will eat whole wheat bread when he can have white bread?) *No one likes the worst of a thing when he can get the best.*

1449. **QUIEN LA FAMA ha perdido, está muerto aunque vivo.** (He who loses his reputation is as good as dead though he may be alive.) *He who takes away my good name takes away my life.*

1450. **QUIEN MAL ANDA, mal acaba.** (He who lives a life of evil dies in evil.) *He who lives by the sword dies by the sword.*

1451. **QUIEN MAL CANTA, bien le suena.** (He who sings badly thinks he sings well.) *Most of us are blind to our own defects.*

1452. **QUIEN MAS CORRE, menos vuela.** (He who runs more flies less.) *The more haste, the less speed.*

1453. QUIEN NADA HACE, nada vale. (He who does nothing is worth nothing.) *A man is known by his works.*

1454. QUIEN NO OYE más que una campana no oye más que un sonido. (He who listens to only one bell hears only one sound.) *There are two sides to every argument.*

1455. QUIEN NO SABE lo que vale no vale nada. (He who does not know how much he is worth is worth nothing.) *Said of someone who does not appreciate himself.*

1456. QUIEN NO SE AVENTURA no pasa la mar. (He who doesn't venture doesn't cross the sea.) *Nothing ventured, nothing gained.*

1457. QUIEN NO TE CONOZCA que te compre. (Let him buy you who doesn't know you.) *Said of someone who is not to be trusted.*

1458. QUIEN NO TIENE suegra ni cuñado, es bien casado. (He who has neither a mother-in-law nor a brother-in-law is well married.) *The best life is a bachelor's life.*

1459. QUIEN PAN menea, pan no desea. (He who makes bread does not crave bread.) *People often desire what they can't have and reject what they already have.*

1460. QUIEN POCO TIENE, poco teme. (He who has little, fears little.) *The less people have, the fewer worries they have.*

1461. QUIEN QUIERE al tronco quiere las hojas de alrededor. (He who likes the trunk likes the leaves surrounding it.) *Love me, love my dog.*

1462. QUIEN QUIERE a Romero quiere a su perro. (He who loves Romero loves his dog.) *Love me, love my dog.*

1463. QUIEN QUITA la ocasión quita el pecado. (He who removes the opportunity gets rid of the sin.) *He who avoids temptation avoids sin.*

1464. QUIEN SABE dos lenguas vale por dos. (He who knows two languages is worth two persons.) *Recommends knowing more than one language.*

1465. QUI EN SIEMBRA vientos recoge tempestades. (He

133

who sows wind, harvests storms.) *As you sow, so shall you reap.*

1466. **¿QUIEN TE la mató que no te la guisó?** (Who dressed it for you and didn't fry it?) *A humorous question asked of one who comes in angry and out of sorts.*

1467. **¿QUIEN TE peló que las orejas no te mochó?** (Who sheared you that didn't cut off your ears?) *Said to someone who just got too short a haircut.*

1468. **QUIEN TODO lo quiere, todo lo pierde.** (He who wants it all, loses it all.) *He who covets all, loses all.*

Río revuelto, ganancia de pescadores.
A muddy river is the fisherman's boon.

1469. **RECAUDO hace cocina, no Catalina.** (It's the provisions that make the meals, not Catalina.) *Money talks.*

1470. **REMIENDA tu costal y te durará un mes.** (Mend your bag and it will last you a month.) *Recommends taking care of one's things.*

1471. **REVERDECER el romero.** (The rosemary becomes green again!) *Said of an adult that is not acting his age.*

1472. **REY muerto, rey puesto.** (The king is dead, the king's replaced.) *Suggests that no one is indispensable and anyone can easily be replaced.*

1473. **RIÑEN las comadres y se dicen las verdades.** (When gossips have a falling out they tell bitter truths.) *Suggests that in anger truth comes out.*

1474. **RIO CRUZADO, santo olvidado.** (The river crossed, the saint forgotten.) *The danger past, the saint forgotten.*

1475. **RIO REVUELTO, ganancia de pescadores.** (A muddy river is the fisherman's boon.) *Much profit can be reaped from confusion.*

1476. RODANDO las piedras se encuentran. (Stones run into each other as they roll along.) *It's a small world.*

1477. ROGAR a Dios por los santos, pero no por tantos. (To pray to God for the saints, but not for so many.) *Censures those who are greedy and who take advantage of others' kindness.*

1478. ROGAR al santo hasta pasar el tranco. (To pray to the saint until the danger is past.) *The danger past, the saint forgotten.*

Se lleva el asno al agua pero no lo hacen beber.
You can lead a horse to water but you can't make him drink.

1479. **SABER ES PODER.** (Knowledge is power.) *Education is power.*

1480. **SAL de tu casa y ven a la mía y pasarás amargo día.** (Leave your house, come to mine, and you will have an awful time.) *Be it ever so humble, there's no place like home.*

1481. **SALE A LA CARA el contento, la enfermedad, la vergüenza.** (Happiness, illness, and shame all show in one's face.) *The face is the mirror of the soul.*

1482. **SALE más barato lo comprado que lo regalado.** (Things bought turn out to be cheaper than things given to us.) *Recommends not accepting favors or gifts because of the ensuing obligation to the donor.*

1483. **SALIR con domingo siete.** (To come out with Sunday the seventh.) *To come out with an impertinent statement, with something foolish, or to put one's foot in it.*

1484. **SALIR con más ojales que botones.** (To come out with more buttonholes than buttons.) *To run short on materials which are needed to complete a job or undertaking.*

1485. **SALIR de Guatemala para entrar en Guatepeor.** (To leave Guatemala [mala-bad] only to enter Guatepeor

[peor-worse].) *To go from the frying pan into the fire.*

1486. **SALTAR del sartén y dar en las brasas.** (To jump from the frying pan and fall in the ashes.) *To go from the frying pan into the fire.*

1487. **SALUD y alegría, belleza crían.** (Health and happiness make one attractive.) *Good health and cheerfulness are reflected in one's appearance.*

1488. **SALVAR los *penes* y malgastar los pesos.** (To save the pennies and mispend the dollars.) *Penny wise and pound foolish.*

1489. **SANAN LLAGAS y no malas palabras.** (The sores get well, the bad words do not.) *Evil tongues wound more deeply than blows.*

1490. **¡SANGRE de venado, todo lo que digas se irá para un lado!** (Blood of a deer, all that you're saying will fall on deaf ears!) *Said to one who we know has slandered us.*

1491. **SANTO NO CONOCIDO, no adorado.** (The saint that is not known is not worshipped.) *Recommends making ourselves known to others.*

1492. **¡SANTO QUE CAGA y mea, el diablo que se lo crea!** (The saint that excretes and voids, let the devil believe him!) *Suggests that a person is not seriously ill if he enjoys body regularity.*

1493. **SANTO que no es visto no es adorado.** (A saint that is not seen is not worshipped.) *One should be present in transactions involving his interests.*

1494. **SANTO TOMAS: ver y creer.** (Like St. Thomas, seeing is believing.) *Seeing is believing.*

1495. **SATISFACCION no pedida, acusación manifiesta.** (An unsolicited apology denotes guilt.) *If a person offers uncalled-for apologies, it's because he has a guilty conscience.*

1496. **SE APURAN más los ordeñadores que los dueños de las vacas.** (The milkers worry more than the owners of the cows.) *Censures those people who play up to* their boss by being overly zealous in protecting his interests.

1497. SE ASUSTAN muertos de degollados. (The dead become frightened with the slain.) *The pot calling the kettle black.*

1498. SECRETO DE DOS, secreto de Dios; secreto de tres, del diablo es. (A secret between two people is God's secret; among three, is the devil's secret.) *What is said among three is soon known by ten.*

1499. SE ESPANTAN los muertos de los degollados. (The dead are scared of the slain.) *The pot calling the kettle black.*

1500. SEGUN LA URRACA es el copete. (As the magpie is, so is the tuft.) *People are treated according to their importance.*

1501. SE JUNTAN más moscas con una gota de miel que con cien de jiel. (More flies gather with a drop of honey than with a hundred drops of bile.) *Tact achieves more than force.*

1502. SE LE CAYO el pan en la miel. (His bread fell in his honey.) *A reference to someone's getting a lucky break or a windfall.*

1503. SE LLEVA el asno al agua pero no lo hacen beber. (You can lead an ass to water but you can't make him drink.) *You can lead a horse to water but you can't make him drink.*

1504. *SEMOS* como los cubos de noria: unos hoy, otros mañana. (We are like old oaken buckets; some today, others tomorrow.) *Life has its ups and downs.*

1505. *SEMOS MEXICANOS,* pero no piones. (We are Mexicans but not peons.) *Suggests that not all persons of Mexican descent should be classed with the common laboring peon.*

1506. SE MURIO el ahijado, se acabó el compadrazgo. (With the godson dead, the copaternity ends.) *Censures those people who sever relations with their friends just because of some loss of interest.*

1507. **SE MURIO el perro, se acabó la rabia.** (With the dog dead, the rabies ends.) *Suggests getting rid of items or things that are useless now that the original reason for having them is no longer present.*

1508. **SEÑAS en el cielo, guerras en el suelo.** (Signs in the sky, wars on the ground.) *A belief that signs in the sky foretell war.*

1509. **SEÑORITA vieja, al infierno por pendeja.** (Old Miss, to Hades for being a fool.) *Censures spinsters for not having married.*

1510. **SE OFRECEN largos y salen cortos.** (They offer their services liberally and come out short.) *Don't offer your services unless you can render them.*

1511. **SE VA la boca donde está el corazón.** (The mouth goes where the heart is.) *People have the name of the person they love on the tip of their tongue.*

1512. **SI A LA VISTA no me agrada, no me aconsejes nada.** (If I don't like it at first sight, don't suggest anything.) *People don't need any advice once they make up their minds.*

1513. **SI A TU HIJO no le das castigo, serás su peor enemigo.** (If you don't correct your child, you will be his worst enemy.) *Spare the rod and spoil the child.*

1514. **SI CON LOBOS andas, a aullar te enseñas.** (Keep company with wolves and you will learn to howl.) *A man is known by the company he keeps.*

1515. **SI DOY, más que tonto soy
si fío, pierdo lo que no es mío;
si presto, me hacen mal gesto,
por lo tanto, desde hoy,
para ahorrarme de este lío,
ni doy, ni fío, ni presto.**

(If I give, I'm more than a fool,
If I sell on credit I lose what's not mine;
If I lend, people are not appreciative,
Therefore, beginning today,
In order to get out of this bind,

140

I will neither give,
Sell on credit, nor lend.)

Neither a borrower nor a lender be.

1516. **SI EL COME de su *troja*, yo como de mi medio almud.** (If he eats from his granary, I'll eat from my half bushel.) *Suggests that no one has any reason to feel superior to another.*

1517. **SI EL CORAZON fuera de acero, no lo venciera el dinero.** (If the heart were made of steel, money could not conquer it.) *Only a very strong person can resist the temptation of money.*

1518. **SI EL OCIO causa tedio, el trabajo es buen remedio.** (If idleness causes boredom, work would surely cure that.) *Work is a good remedy for boredom.*

1519. **SI EL VINO te tiene loco, déjalo poquito a poco.** (If wine is driving you crazy, leave it little by little.) *Recommends getting rid of a bad habit before it gets hold of you.*

1520. **SIEMPRE CORRIENDO y llegando tarde.** (Always on the run and always arriving late.) *Censures people who are always late for appointments, work, etc., due to lack of organization.*

1521. **SIEMPRE EL POBRE llega tarde aunque madrugue.** (The poor man always arrives late, even if he gets up early.) *A complaint on the part of the poor who feel the pangs of discrimination.*

1522. **SIEMPRE EN LO AJENO cae la mancha.** (Borrowed things always get soiled.) *Suggests being careful with borrowed things or not borrowing them, as something always happens to them.*

1523. **SIEMPRE NOS PARECEN más maduras las peras del vecino.** (The neighbor's pears always seem riper.) *The grass always looks greener on the other side of the fence.*

1524. **SI EN TU TIERRA apellido, en la ajena tu vestido.** (If you're important at home because of your name, it's

141

your clothes that count away from home.) *Clothes make the man.*

1525. **SIETE DIAS tiene la semana, lo que no puedas hacer hoy, déjalo para mañana.** (A week has seven days; whatever you cannot do today, leave for tomorrow.) *A humorous parody of another proverb which suggests not leaving for tomorrow what you can do today.*

1526. **SI LA ENVIDIA fuera *tinta*, todos tiñeran con ella.** (If envy were dye, we would all dye with it.) *Suggests that it is hard not to feel envious of others.*

1527. **SI LOS LOCOS usaran coronas, todos fuéramos reyes.** (If madmen wore crowns, we'd all be kings.) *There's a little of the madman in all of us.*

1528. **SI ME QUIERE con esta cara, si no, vaya.** (If you like me with this face, all right; if not go your way.) *Suggests taking people for what they are.*

1529. **SIN AJO se guisa mi olla, y sin su calor se cuece.** (My pot does all right without garlic and it cooks without your fire.) *Censures people for not minding their own business.*

1530. **SI NO HUBIERA malos gustos, ¿qué fuera de los feos?** (What would become of the homely if it weren't for poor tastes?) *There's no accounting for tastes.*

1531. **SI NO PUEDES lo que quieras, quiere lo que puedes.** (If you can't get what you want, be content with what you have.) *Suggests being happy with what little you have.*

1532. **SI NO TIENES DINERO en la bolsa, ten miel en la boca.** (If you have no money in your purse, have honey in your mouth.) *Lip service sometimes accomplishes much.*

1533. **SIN PADRE ni madre, ni perro que le ladre.** (Without parents or a dog to bark at him.) *Said of persons who seem to be totally without any friends or relatives.*

1534. **SI OYES un mal son, avísale a talón.** (If you hear a bad sound, advise your heels.) *Recommends being on the alert for signs of danger.*

1535. **SI PUEDES SOLO, no esperes a otro.** (If you can do it alone, don't wait for anyone.) *Recommends not asking favors unless it is absolutely necessary.*

1536. **SI QUIERES ACERTAR, cásate con tu igual.** (If you want to succeed, marry your equal.) *Suggests marrying one's equal.*

1537. **SI QUIERES BUENA FAMA, no te halle el sol en la cama.** (If you want a good name, don't let the sun find you in bed.) *Early to bed and early to rise, makes a man healthy, wealthy, and wise.*

1538. **SI QUIERES CONOCER a Andrés, vive con él un mes.** (If you want to know Andrew, live with him a month.) *Suggests getting close to a person in order to know him better.*

1539. **SI QUIERES FORTUNA y fama, levántate de mañana.** (If you want fortune and fame, get up early.) *The early bird catches the worm.*

1540. **SI QUIERES PASAR mal día, deja tu casa y vente a la mía.** (If you want a bad time, leave your house and come to mine.) *Be it ever so humble, there's no place like home.*

1541. **SI QUIERES QUE OTRO se ría, cuenta tus penas a María.** (If you want others to laugh, tell your troubles to someone.) *Suggests keeping one's sorrows to ourselves.*

1542. **SI QUIERES QUE SEPAN lo que eres, cuéntaselo a las mujeres.** (If you want people to know what you are, tell it to women.) *Suggests that women are gossips.*

1543. **SI QUIERES SABER quién es, vive con él un mes.** (If you want to know who he is, live with him for a month.) *We get to know people by close association with them.*

1544. **SI QUIERES SER SERVIDO, sírvete a ti mismo.** (If you want to be served, serve yourself.) *If you want something done well, do it yourself.*

1545. **SI QUIERES VIVIR sano, hazte viejo temprano.** (If you want to live a healthy life, become old earlier.) *Suggests taking care of yourself while you are young.*

1546. SI RESPETAS a tus mayores, te respetan tus menores.
(If you respect your elders, you get respect from the
youngsters.) *Suggests honoring your elders.*

1547. SI TE VI no me acuerdo y si te conocí no sé dónde. (If
I saw you, I don't remember, and if I met you I don't
know where.) *A way of telling someone you don't
know him from Adam.*

1548. SI TIENES CORAJE, anda al trabajo que se te baje.
(If you're angry, go to work and cool off.) *Suggests
working off anger.*

1549. SI TU MAL tiene remedio, ¿para qué te apuras? (If
your sickness can be cured, why worry?) *Recommends
that one not worry unduly over problems that can be
solved.*

1550. SOBRE GUSTOS no hay disputa. (There is no argument concerning tastes.) *There's no accounting for
tastes.*

1551. SOBRE GUSTOS no hay nada escrito. (There is nothing written on tastes.) *Every man to his taste.*

1552. SOBRE PADRE no hay compadre. (No closer friend
than one's father.) *Blood is thicker than water.*

1553. SOLDADO raso no repela. (The buck private does not
grumble.) *Subordinates, because of their position, must
do menial work.*

1554. SOLO DIOS sabe para quién trabajas. (Only God
knows for whom you work.) *One does the toil and
another benefits from it.*

**1555. SOLO EL QUE CARGA el cajón sabe lo que pesa el
muerto.** (Only he who carries the coffin knows what
the corpse weighs.) *Only he who wears the shoe knows
where it pinches.*

**1556. SOLO EL QUE CARGA el morral sabe lo que tiene
dentro.** (Only he who carries the horse's food bag
knows what's in it.) *Only he who wears the shoe knows
where it pinches.*

1557. SOLO EL QUE CARGA el saco sabe lo que lleva den-

144

tro. (Only he who carries the bag knows what's in it.) *Only he who wears the shoe knows where it pinches.*

1558. **SOL que mucho madruga, poco dura.** (The sun that rises early does not last.) *Fires lit early soon burn out.*

1559. **SON más las echadas que las que están poniendo.** (The brooding hens outnumber those that are laying.) *Censures people that brag or boast.*

1560. **SON más los truenos que 'l agua.** (There's more thunder than rain.) *Much ado about nothing.*

1561. **SON muchos los diablos y poco 'l agua bendita.** (There are too many devils and there's not enough holy water.) *Said when there is not enough to go around.*

1562. **SOPLAR y sorber no pueden a un tiempo ser.** (Blowing and sipping cannot occur at the same time.) *You cannot do two things at once.*

1563. **SUEGRO y yerno, ni en el infierno.** (Father-in-law and son-in-law, not even in hell.) *Emphasizes how difficult it is to get along with one's father-in-law or son-in-law.*

1564. **SUERTE te dé Dios, que el saber poco importa.** (God grant you luck, because being knowledgeable is of little value.) *Good fortune is better than knowledge.*

1565. **SUFRE por saber y trabaja por tener.** (Suffer to learn and work to obtain wealth.) *Suggests that knowledge and wealth do not come easily.*

Tal el padre, tal el hijo.
Like father, like son.

1566. TAL EL AMO, tal el criado. (Like the master, like the servant.) *Like begets like.*

1567. TAL EL PADRE, tal el hijo. (Like the father, like the son.) *Like father, like son.*

1568. TAL para cual. (Tit for tat.) *You get what you give.*

1569. TAMBIEN DE DOLOR se canta cuando llorar no se puede. (One can sing of one's sorrow when crying is impossible.) *Suggests that happiness may be put on.*

1570. TAMBIEN la vista engaña. (The eye also deceives.) *Appearances are deceiving.*

1571. TAMBIEN para los pinos hay hacha. (Even for pine trees there's an axe.) *The bigger they come the harder they fall.*

1572. TAN LEJOS de ojos, tan lejos de corazón. (So far from the eye, so distant from the heart.) *Out of sight, out of mind.*

1573. TAN SINVERGÜENZA es el pinto como el colorado. (The mottled is as shameless as the red one.) *Suggests that it is hard to choose between two dishonest people.*

1574. TANTAS veces va el cántaro al agua hasta que se queda dentro. (The pitcher goes to the well so often that eventually it falls in.) *The law of averages usually takes its toll.*

1575. TANTO LE PICAN al burro hasta que por fin respinga. (Provoked once too often, the donkey will buck and kick.) *There is a limit to one's patience.*

1576. TANTO PECA el que mata la vaca como el que tiene la pata. (He who kills the cow sins as much as he who has the leg.) *Accomplices are as guilty as offenders.*

1577. TANTO QUIERES saber hasta que lo echas a perder. (You want to know so much that you end up spoiling it.) *He who covets all, loses all.*

1578. TANTO QUISO el indio al burro hasta que le arrancó la cola. (The Indian so loved his donkey that he finally tore off his tail.) *An indulgent parent often spoils his child.*

1579. TANTO tienes, tanto vales. (You have so much, you're worth that much.) *A belief that people are worth what they have in the bank.*

1580. TANTO VA el cántaro al agua hasta que se quiebra. (The pitcher goes to the well so many times that finally it breaks.) *The law of averages usually takes its toll.*

1581. TE ASUSTAS con la mortaja y te abrazas del muerto. (You get frightened with the shroud and hug the corpse.) *Censures those who feign horror at others' minor shortcomings and at the same time overlook their own more serious ones.*

1582. TE CASASTE, te fregaste. (You got married, you got yourself hooked.) *Emphasizes that with marriage comes the loss of a carefree life.*

1583. TE DAN la mano y quieres el pie. (They give you their hand and you take their foot.) *Give an inch and they'll take a mile.*

1584. TIEMPO perdido los santos lo lloran. (The saints weep over lost time.) *Suggests that it is a sin to waste time.*

147

1585. TIENE más Dios que darnos que nosotros que pedirle. (God has more to offer than we could ever ask for.) *Emphasizes the greatness of God.*

1586. TIRAN más tetas que carretas. (Breasts have more influence than ox carts.) *Women have a strong influence on men.*

1587. TIRAR PEDRADAS al matorral después de conejo ido. (They throw stones at the brush after the rabbit's gone.) *Closing the barn door after the horse is stolen.*

1588. TODAVIA no tienen vaca y ya pelean por la leche. (They don't even have a cow and they're fighting over the milk.) *Don't count your chickens before they are hatched.*

1589. TODAVIA VEN LA TEMPESTAD y no se hincan. (Even with the storm upon them they don't kneel down to pray.) *Said of people who are surrounded by misfortune but continue pushing their luck.*

1590. TODO CABE en un costal, sabiéndolo acomodar. (Everything fits in a bag if you know how to get it in.) *Suggests being organized in order to accomplish something successfully.*

1591. TODO CAE en el dedo malo. (Everything falls on the sore thumb.) *When it rains, it pours.*

1592. TODO LO CONSERVA el alcohol, menos el empleo. (Alcohol preserves everything except one's job.) *A warning that alcohol can cause us to lose our jobs.*

1593. TODO saldrá en la lavada. (Everything will come out in the wash.) *When the truth is told everything is known.*

1594. TODOS HIJOS de Dios o todos entenados. (We are all God's children or all stepchildren.) *Suggests equal treatment for everyone.*

1595. TODO VALE en el nombre de Dios. (Everything is valid in God's name.) *Even the devil quotes the scripture.*

1596. TRAERLE a uno de Herodes a Pilatos. (To have one going from Herod to Pilate.) *To have one going from pillar to post.*

1597. TRAS de cuernos, palos. (After making a cuckold out of you, they beat you.) *Adding insult to injury.*

1598. TRAS de la cruz está el diablo. (Behind the cross the devil lurks.) *Censures hypocrites.*

1599. TU HIJO cuando quieras, tu hija cuando puedas. (Your son, whenever you wish; your daughter, whenever you can.) *Implies that it's easier to marry off one's son than one's daughter.*

Una llave de oro abre cualquier puerta.
A gold key opens any door.

1600. UNA ABEJA no hace colmena. (One bee does not make a beehive.) *One exception does not make a rule.*

1601. UNA BUENA ACCION es la mejor oración. (One good action is the best prayer.) *Actions speak louder than words.*

1602. UNA CAMINATA de cien millas se comienza con el primer paso. (A hundred-mile journey begins with the first step.) *You have to start somewhere.*

1603. UNA COSA APURADA es mal hecha y desbaratada. (A thing done hastily is done badly and easily falls apart.) *Haste makes waste.*

1604. UNA COSA es el amor y el negocio es otra cosa. (Love is one thing and business another.) *Don't mix business with pleasure.*

1605. UNA COSA ES LA AMISTAD y otra cosa es "no la friegues." (Friendship is one thing and taking advantage is another.) *Don't take advantage of someone's friendship.*

1606. UNA COSA ES PROMETER y otra es cumplir. (To promise is one thing, to fulfill the promise is another.) *Don't promise to do something if you can't do it.*

150

1607. **UNA GOLONDRINA no hace verano.** (One swallow does not a summer make.) *One exception doesn't make a rule.*

1608. **UNA HORMIGA sola no hace verano.** (A single ant does not make a summer.) *One exception doesn't make a rule.*

1609. **UNA LLAVE de oro abre cualquier puerta.** (A gold key opens any door.) *Money talks.*

1610. **UNA MALA CABRA descompone un ganado entero.** (One bad goat spoils a whole flock.) *One rotten apple spoils a whole barrelful.*

1611. **UNA MALA RES descompone un rodeo.** (A bad steer spoils an entire rodeo.) *One rotten apple spoils a whole barrelful.*

1612. **UNA MANO lava la otra y las dos lavan la cara.** (One hand washes the other and both wash the face.) *Recommends cooperation in helping one another.*

1613. **UNA MANZANA podrida echa a perder a las demás.** (One rotten apple spoils all the rest.) *One rotten apple spoils a barrelful.*

1614. **UNA MANZANA PODRIDA echa a perder un cajón.** (A rotten apple spoils a whole box full.) *One rotten apple spoils a barrelful.*

1615. **UNA OVEJA mala descompone un rebaño.** (One bad sheep spoils a flock.) *One rotten apple spoils a barrelful.*

1616. **UNA PUNTADA a tiempo salva un ciento.** (A stitch in time saves a hundred.) *A stitch in time saves nine.*

1617. **UÑAS de gato y túnico de beato.** (Claws of a cat and tunic of a pious person.) *Said of a hypocrite or a wolf in sheep's clothing.*

1618. **UN BIEN con otro se paga.** (One good deed is repaid with another.) *One good turn deserves another.*

1619. **UN BIEN con un mal se paga.** (One good deed is paid with evil.) *Censures those who repay a good turn with ungratefulness.*

1620. **UN BUEN TRAJE encubre un ruin linaje.** (Nice clothing conceals low lineage.) *Clothes make the man.*

1621. **UN CABELLO de mujer tira más que cien yuntas de bueyes.** (A woman's hair has more influence than a hundred teams of oxen.) *Women have a strong influence on men.*

1622. **UN CLAVO saca otro clavo.** (One nail pulls out another.) *Like cures like.*

1623. **UN GRANO no hace granero pero ayuda a su compañero.** (One grain does not make a granary, but it helps its companions.) *Many a mickle makes a muckle.*

1624. **UN GRITO a tiempo saca un cimarrón del monte.** (A shout in time gets a stray animal out of the woods.) *A stitch in times saves nine.*

1625. **UN LOBO no muerde a otro.** (One wolf does not bite another wolf.) *Thieves do not steal from thieves.*

1626. **UN LOCO hace *cien*.** (One madman makes a hundred.) *Arguing with a fool shows there are more fools.*

1627. **UN MAL con un bien se paga.** (A wrong is repaid with a good turn.) *To err is human, to forgive, divine.*

1628. **UN MAL IDO, otro venido.** (One ill gone, another takes its place.) *Misfortunes never come singly.*

1629. **UN MAL LLAMA a otro.** (One ill attracts another.) *When it rains, it pours.*

1630. **UNO CALIENTA para que otro coma.** (One man heats the food for another to eat it.) *One man toils and another reaps the benefit.*

1631. **UNO COME la fruta aceda y otro tiene la dentera.** (One eats the spoiled fruit and another becomes ill.) *Suggests that one often has to pay for his ancestors' faults.*

1632. **UNO CORRE la liebre y otro es el que la alcanza.** (One chases the hare and another catches it.) *One man toils and another reaps the benefit.*

1633. **UNO DICE el bayo y otro el que lo monta.** (The bay horse says one thing and the rider another.) *Suggests that the employee says one thing and the employer another.*

1634. **UNO EN EL SACO y otro en el sobaco.** (One thing in the bag and another under your arm.) *Be prepared.*

1635. **UNO ES el de la fama y otro el que carga la lana.** (One gets the fame and another cards the wool.) *One does the dirty work and another gets the fame.*

1636. **UNO PIENSA el bayo y otro el que lo monta.** (The bay horse thinks one thing and its rider another.) *Suggests that the employee says one thing and the employer another.*

1637. **UNOS CARDAN la lana y otros agarran la fama.** (Some card the wool and others get the credit.) *One does the dirty work and another gets the fame.*

1638. **UNOS CORREN la liebre y otros sin correr la alcanzan.** (Some chase the hare and others catch it without running.) *Some people are successful without even trying.*

1639. **UNOS DE PEDIR se cansan y otros sin pedir les dan.** (Some get tired of begging and others can get without begging.) *Some people get all the breaks.*

1640. **UNOS NACEN con estrella y otros nacen estrellados.** (Some are born with a star while others are born seeing stars.) *Some people are born lucky, some unlucky.*

1641. **UNOS NACEN de pie y otros de cabeza.** (Some are born feet first and others head first.) *Some people are born lucky, some unlucky.*

1642. **UNOS PORQUE TIENEN y otros porque no tienen.** (Some because they have and others because they do not.) *Suggests that people are never satisfied with what they have.*

1643. **UNOS VAN al duelo y otros al buñuelo.** (Some people go to the funeral, others to the food.) *Some people go to funerals not out of sympathy, but for the food.*

1644. **UN PADRE para cien hijos pero no cien hijos para**

un padre. (One parent for a hundred children but not a hundred children for one parent.) *The love of parents for their children is greater than the love of children for their parents.*

1645. **UN PAJARO en la mano es mejor que dos en el árbol.** (A bird in the hand is better than two on the tree.) *A bird in the hand is worth two in the bush.*

1646. **UN PETATE es buen colchón para aquél que lo tumba el sueño.** (A mat makes a fine mattress for him who is really sleepy.) *The best mattress is a good sleep.*

1647. **UN SOLO GOLPE no tumba un roble.** (A single blow does not fell an oak tree.) *Rome wasn't built in a day.*

1648. **UN VIEJO AMIGO es el mejor espejo.** (An old friend is one's best mirror.) *One's best mirror is an old friend.*

Víbora que chilla no pica.
A snake that hisses does not bite.

1649. **VALE más adorada de viejo que esclava de joven.** (Better to be loved by an old man than enslaved by a young one.) *Better to be an old man's darling than a young man's slave.*

1650. **VALE más algo que nada.** (Better a little something than nothing at all.) *Half a loaf is better than none.*

1651. **VALE más año tardío que vacío.** (Better a late harvest than a fruitless one.) *Half a loaf is better than none.*

1652. **VALE más arrear que no la carga llevar.** (Better to be in the driver's seat than to carry the load.) *Better to give instructions as to how to do a thing than to have to do it.*

1653. **VALE más bien quedada que mal casada.** (Better to have stayed single than to have made a bad marriage.) *A life alone without worries is better than a miserable married life.*

1654. **VALE más cabeza de ratón que cola de león.** (Better the head of a mouse than the tail of a lion.) *Better a big frog in a little pond than a little frog in a large pond.*

1655. **VALE más callar que locamente hablar.** (Better to keep silent than to babble.) *Silence is golden.*

155

1656. VALE más comprado que regalado. (Better bought than received as a gift.) *It is better to pay for one's things than to be indebted.*

1657. VALE más el peor arreglo que el mejor pleito. (Better a bad compromise than a good lawsuit.) *A bad settlement is always better than the best lawsuit.*

1658. VALE más frijoles con hambre que *chinitos* con manteca. (Better beans with a good appetite than pork with all its lard.) *A bird in the hand is worth two in the bush.*

1659. VALE más gota de sangre que arroba de amistad. (A drop of blood is dearer than a gallon of friendship.) *Blood is thicker than water.*

1660. VALE más hoy que mañana. (Better today than tomorrow.) *A bird in the hand is worth two in the bush.*

1661. VALE más llegar a tiempo que ser convidado. (It is better to arrive on time than to be invited.) *Said by persons who happen to arrive unexpectedly just as a family is sitting down to a meal.*

1662. VALE más maña que fuerza. (Resourcefulness is better than strength.) *Brain over brawn.*

1663. VALE más onza de prudencia que libra de ciencia. (An ounce of prudence is worth a pound of science.) *An ounce of prevention is worth a pound of cure.*

1664. VALE más pájaro en mano que *cien* volando. (A bird in the hand is worth a hundred on the wing.) *A bird in the hand is worth two in the bush.*

1665. VALE más paso que dure que no que apresure. (Better an even pace than one that goes too fast.) *Slow but steady wins the race.*

1666. VALE más perro vivo que león muerto. (Better a dog alive than a lion dead.) *Better a live coward than a dead hero.*

1667. VALE más poco y bien ganado que mucho y enzoquetado. (Better a little earned with honesty than a great deal gained with dishonesty.) *Honesty is the best policy.*

156

1668. **VALE más querer a un perro que a una ingrata mujer.** (Better to love a dog than a disagreeable woman.) *Expresses the opinion that a woman's love is not always as faithful as that of a dog.*

1669. **VALE más ratón vivo que león muerto.** (Better a live mouse than a dead lion.) *Better a live coward than a dead hero.*

1670. **VALE más saber que tener.** (Better to have knowledge than possessions.) *Knowledge is better than material possessions.*

1671. **VALE más solo que mal acompañado.** (Better to be alone than in bad company.) *You're judged by the company you keep.*

1672. **VALE más sufrir la injusticia que ser injusto.** (Better to suffer injustice than to be unjust.) *To do injustice is more disgraceful than to suffer it.*

1673. **VALE más una onza de amistad que una libra de hostilidad.** (Better an ounce of friendship than a pound of hostility.) *Better to make friends than enemies.*

1674. **VALE más una onza de libertad que quinientas libras de oro.** (Better an ounce of freedom than five hundred pounds of gold.) *Freedom is priceless.*

1675. **VALE más un muchacho roto que un viejo con pantalones.** (Better a boy in rags than a well-dressed old man.) *Shows preference for youth over age.*

1676. **VALE más un "toma" que dos "te daré."** (Better one "Here, take" than two "I shall give.") *A bird in the hand is worth two in the bush.*

1677. **VALE más vecino cerca que pariente lejos.** (Better a neighbor near than a relative afar.) *A good neighbor can often be of more help in an emergency than a close relative who lives far away from us.*

1678. **VALE más vivo barbón que muerto *resurado*.** (Better bearded but alive than dead and shaven.) *Better a live coward than a dead hero.*

1679. **VALE más zapato malo en el pie que bueno en la**

mano. (Better a poor shoe on the foot than a good shoe in the hand.) *A bird in the hand is worth two in the bush.*

1680. **VAMOS a ver, dijo el ciego.** ("Let's see," said the blind man.) *An expression used instead of just saying "Let's see."*

1681. **VANSE LOS AMORES y quedan los dolores.** (The lover gone, the ache remains.) *The bonds of love remain after parting.*

1682. **VER es creer.** (To see is to believe.) *Seeing is believing.*

1683. **VIBORA que chilla no pica.** (A snake that hisses does not bite.) *His bark is worse than his bite.*

1684. **VIDA sin amigos, muerte sin testigos.** (A life without friends means a death without witnesses.) *He who has no friends dies alone.*

1685. **VIEJO está Pedro para cabrero.** (Peter is too old to be a goatherd.) *Advises against doing things that will harm us because of our age.*

1686. **VIEJO que se cura, cien años dura.** (The old man that takes care of his health lives a hundred years.) *Recommends taking care of yourself if you want to be healthy.*

1687. **VIENES a deseo, hueles a poleo.** (If you come when you're wanted, you smell of mint.) *A welcome guest is well received.*

1688. **VISTEME despacio que tengo prisa.** (Dress me slowly, for I am in a hurry.) *Haste makes waste.*

1689. **VOZ del pueblo, voz del cielo.** (The voice of the people, the voice of heaven.) *The voice of the people is the voice of God.*

Ya que la casa se quema, vamos a calen-tarnos.
Since the house is burning, let us warm our-selves.

1690. **YA comí, ya me voy, como dijo el indio.** (I've already eaten; I'm leaving.) *Censures those who desert their friends when no more favors are forthcoming.*

1691. **YA CONOZCO a la Rafela, no me la ponderen tanto.** (I already know Rafela, you don't have to exaggerate.) *When one knows a situation well, there is no need for someone to exaggerate.*

1692. **YA está muy viejo Pedro pa cabrero.** (Peter is much too old for a goatherd.) *Suggests not doing things one shouldn't because of advanced age.*

1693. **YA LO PARIMOS, ahora hay que criarlo.** (We gave him birth, now let's raise him.) *Suggests facing the con-sequences despite bad judgment.*

1694. **YA QUE LA CASA se quema, vamos a calentarnos.** (Since the house is burning, let us warm ourselves.) *Suggests making the best of a bad situation.*

1695. **YA *servites*, María, vete, María.** (You've done your part, Mary, go away, Mary.) *The goods received, the donor forgotten.*

1696. **YO no le suelto la cola aunque me cague la mano.** (I won't let go of the tail even though I get my hand soiled.) *Suggests being steadfast in one's work and car-rying it out to the end.*

Zorra vieja no cae en la trampa.
An old fox doesn't fall in the trap.

1697. ZORRA vieja no cae en la trampa. (An old fox doesn't fall in the trap.) *You can't catch old birds with chaff.*

SELECTED READINGS

Bergua, José. *Refranero español*. Madrid: Ediciones Ibéricas [1961].

Brown, Lawrence K. *A Thesaurus of Spanish Idioms and Everyday Language*. New York: The Marcel Rodd Co., 1945.

Campa, A.L. *Sayings and Riddles in New Mexico*. Vol. 8, no. 2. University of New Mexico Language Series. Albuquerque: University of New Mexico Press, 1937.

Cerda, Gilberto, et al. *Vocabulario español de Texas*. Austin: University of Texas Press, 1970.

Cobos, Rubén. *A Dictionary of New Mexico and Southern Colorado Spanish*. Santa Fe: Museum of New Mexico Press, 1983.

Collins, John. *A Dictionary of Spanish Proverbs*. London: S. Brooke, n.d.

Davidoff, Henry. *Treasury of Proverbs*. New York: Grosset & Dunlap, 1946.

Espinosa, A.M. "New Mexican Spanish Folk Lore. IV Proverbs." *Journal of American Folklore* 26, no. 100 (April-June 1913).

————. *Estudios sobre el español de Nuevo Méjico*. Buenos Aires: Instituto de Filología, 1942.

Galloway, Clifford H. *The Book of Spanish Proverbs*. New York: Spanish-American Printing Co., 1944.

Jiménez, A. *Picardía mexicana*. México: Libro Mex. Ed., 1961.

Kercheville, F.M. *A Preliminary Glossary of New Mexican Spanish*. Vol. 5, no. 3. University of New Mexico Language Series. Albuquerque: University of New Mexico Press, 1934.

Kin, David. *Dictionary of American Proverbs*. New York: Philosophical Library, 1955.

Lea, Aurora Lucero White. *Literary Folklore of the Hispanic Southwest*. San Antonio: Naylor Press [1953].

Malaret, Augusto. *Diccionario de americanismos*. Buenos Aires: Academia Argentina de Letras, 1942.

Martínez Kleiser, Luis. *Refranero ideológico español*. Madrid: Real Academia Española, 1953.

Mendoza, Iñigo López de. *Proverbios*. Madrid: Victoriano Suárez, 1928.

Opdyke, George Howard. *The World's Best Proverbs*. Chicago: Laird and Lee, n.d.

Rael, Juan B. *Cuentos españoles de Colorado y Nuevo Méjico*, 2 vols. 2d rev. ed. Santa Fe: Museum of New Mexico Press, 1977.

Rubio, Darío. *La anarquía del lenguaje en la América Española*. México, 1925.

————. *Refranes, proverbios y dichos y dicharachos mexicanos.* México: Ediciones A.P. Márquez, 1940.

Santamaría, Francisco J. *Diccionario de mejicanismos.* Ed. Porrúa. México, 1959.

————. *Diccionario general de americanismos.* Edited by Pedro Robredo. México, 1942.

Taylor, Archer. *The Proverb.* Hatboro: Folklore Associates, 1962.

Toor, Frances. *A Treasury of Mexican Folkways.* New York: Crown Publishers, 1962.

INDICE

*(Los números corresponden al número
del refrán.)*

Barriga, 131
Barrigón, 430, 545, 561
Beato, 192
Belleza, 132
Bien, 302, 431, 432, 433, 817, 818, 1076, 1161, 1206
Blanca-trigueña, 1276
Boca cerrada, moscas, 141, 226, 521, 689, 690, 691
Bocado, 1239
Boda-tornaboda, 1218
Bollo, 1166
Bolsa, 142
Borracho, 1080, 1194, 1220
Bota, 65
Botones, 732
Brazo, 1190
Bueno, 813
Buenos, 116
Buey, 3, 4, 21, 44, 151, 412, 601, 625, 705, 1057
Bulto, 659
Burra, 854, 1314, 1315
Burro, 5, 136, 152, 153, 571, 736, 1290

C

Caballada, 73
Caballo, 6, 154, 155, 156, 157
Cabeza de ratón, 1103
Cabresto, 435
Caída, 291
Calabaza caliente, 186
Calaveras, 971
Calidad, 373
Callar, 187, 522, 1655
Calle, 51, 188
Camarón, 436
Camino, 15, 533, 1187
Cana, 190, 936
Candela, 175
Candil, 191
Cantar, 523, 578
Cántaro, 1574
Capillita, 8
Cara, 77, 192, 193, 213
Carácter, 68, 162, 429, 561, 597,

599, 601, 699, 700, 702, 703, 774, 855, 964, 1145, 1165, 1276
Carbón-brasa, 438
Cárcel-cama, 711
Caridad, 191, 434, 817, 860
Carne-lomo, 272
Carta-firmar, 1209
Casa, 178, 196, 199, 285, 520, 694, 695, 696, 697, 698, 699, 700, 701, 702, 703, 863
Casado, 195, 961
Casamiento, 197, 198
Casarse, 91, 544, 641, 1536, 1582
Casorio, 1238
Castigo, 376
Cebolla, 240
'Cemitas, 24, 1327
Cencerro, 3
Centavos, 286
Chamaco, 268
Chango, 159
Chencha, 60
Chiche, 173
Chiflar, pinole, 1279
Chile, 986
Chillidos, 17
Chisme, 439
Ciego, 1245, 1257, 1680
Cielo, 269
Cirio, 334
Clavo, 289
Cocinera, 36
Cocinero, 54
Codicia, 669, 867
Cojear, 608
Cojera, 704
Col, 632, 724
Colchón, 966, 1240
Colmillo, 5
Comadres, 275
Comal, 442, 443
Comer, 18, 203, 204, 223, 305, 524, 803, 1202
Comida, 205
Compadre, 215
Compañía, 205, 216, 369
Cómplice, 988
Comprar, 277, 1078, 1226, 1656

164

Espejo, 424, 1242
Esperar, 551
Esperanza, 879, 942
Equivocarse, 663
Estorbar, 802
Estornudar, 177
Estreñido, 457
Estupidez, 1035, 1043

F

Fama, 25, 251, 1635
Familiaridad, 881
Favor, 454, 458, 571, 745, 746, 747, 1077, 1535
Fe perdida, 752
Fea, 950, 1167
Feria, 180
Fiar, 557, 979
Fierro, 194
Fiesta, 231, 1011
Fiestecita, 8
Flojera, 882
Flojo, 459
Fortuna, 629
Fray Modesto, 1293
Freír, 32, 48
Frío, 378
Función, 12
Fruta prohibida, 883

G

Gallina, 884, 1284
Gallo, 547, 653, 1298
Gana, 398
Ganancias, 1185
Ganar, 981
Garrapata, 4
Gastar, 1211
Gatos, 26, 234, 260, 335, 416, 461, 570, 826, 827, 1256
Gavilán, 395, 413
Gente, 885
Gloria, 227, 238, 633
Goloso, 309
Gracia, 1077
Granjear, 1004, 1026
Grano, 310

Grulla, 120
Guajolote, 9
Guajolotito, 10, 119
Guatemala-Guatepeor, 1485
Guayabe, 1195
Guerra, 35
Gustos, 14, 311, 626, 726, 785, 806, 807, 1550, 1551

H

Habas, 692, 721
Hábito, 1524
Hablar, 111, 464, 486, 506, 510, 559, 560, 590, 591, 1136
Hablador, 185
Hacer, 20, 995, 1018, 1020, 1525
Hacerla, pagarla, 568
Hallar, 980
Hambre, 2, 465, 466, 894
Hatajo, 1230
Hecho, pecho, 59
Hermosa, 441
Herodes-Pilatos, 1596
Herrero, 694
Hiel, 141
Hierro, 31, 513
Hígado, 1002
Higos, 74
Hijo, 93, 105, 337, 567, 1036
Hipocresía, 872
Hipócrita, 672
Hojas, 943
Honor, 733
Honra, 859
Honradez, 887
Horas antes, 1081
Huaraches, 69
Hueso, 657
Huéspedes, 140

I

Idolatrar, 658
Indio, 261, 1195, 1283
Indirectas, 367
Injuria, 896
Intenciones, 475
Interés, 476

Ir, 211, 282

INDEX

*(The numbers refer to the number of
the proverb.)*

Brave, 1154
Bread, 2, 24, 96, 200, 496, 953, 1121, 1325, 1326, 1327, 1328, 1329, 1339, 1459
Breaks, 1639, 1640, 1641
Breasts, 744, 1070, 1586
Burnt, 461
Business, 60, 153, 171, 723, 725, 799, 940, 1003, 1299, 1405, 1529
Butcher, 17
Buying-selling, 114, 277, 1655
Bygones, 1016

C

Calamity, 266
Call, 18
Candle, 334
Care, 823, 1440, 1545, 1686
Castrated, 195
Cat, 26, 192, 260, 335, 767, 768, 769, 770, 771, 772
Cattle tick, 4
Certainty, 1187
Chaff, 1697
Chain, 435, 469, 931
Change, 1408
Chapel, 8
Chaperone, 22
Character, 68, 162, 429, 561, 596, 597, 598, 599, 600, 601, 698, 774, 855, 964, 1145, 1165, 1276
Characteristics, 694, 698
Charity, 191, 434, 817, 860
Charms, 441, 744, 1251
Cheap things, 994
Cheated, 1283
Chew, 587
Chickens, 325, 830, 1158, 1169, 1185, 1588
Children, 527, 640, 829, 831, 1035, 1036, 1037, 1038, 1269, 1444, 1578
Chip (off old block), 354, 355
Choosers, 108
Claims, 804
Cleanliness, 891
Clothes, 138, 150, 214, 684, 933, 934, 1524

Commitment, 745
Common, 564
Companions, 1267
Company, 116, 216, 239, 369, 517, 736, 848, 972, 1326, 1514, 1671
Complaining, 1258
Compliment, 244, 1227
Compromise, 1079, 1083
Conceited, 555
Connections, 1428
Conscience, 1495
Consciousness, 218
Consequences, 1020, 1205, 1693
Constitution, 1322
Contempt, 687
Contentment, 109, 131, 779
Convenience, 145
Cooks, 54, 130, 1133
Cooperation, 1612
Co-signing, 758
Courage, 794
Courtesy, 244, 1154
Covet, 669, 867, 1468, 1577
Cowbell, 3
Cow, 270, 705
Cowards, 581, 977, 1097, 1666, 1669, 1678
Craftsman, 708
Credit, 979
Crime, 915
Criticism, 593, 1196, 1199, 1201, 1202, 1260
Cross, 356
Crows, 250
Cuckold, 595, 600
Cup, 315
Customs, 13

D

Dancer, 1434
Danger, 1355, 1474, 1478, 1534
Darling, 1649
Deaf, 498, 674
Death, 16, 316, 321, 971, 1244
Debts, 618
Deception, 242
Deeds, 792
Defects, 156, 415, 965, 995, 1001,

1164, 1168, 1418, 1451
Delay, 709
Demotion, 297
Dependence, 19, 226
Despair, 551
Destitute, 410
Devil, 137, 258, 338, 717, 788, 789
Diarrhea, 457
Dice, 982
Die, 46
Differences, 987
Diligence, 875
Disappointment, 233, 840
Discontent, 1237
Discord, 407
Discretion, 816
Discrimination, 155, 1195, 1521
Discussion, 789, 885
Dishonest person, 1573
Disinterest, 818
Disposition, 598
Dissipation, 1182
Distributing, 1327
Distrust, 1457
Dissuaded, 1190
Dividing, sharing, 621
Do unto others, 229, 1212
Dog, 8, 9, 10, 12, 29, 119, 166, 207, 502, 503, 1363, 1364, 1365, 1366, 1435, 1461, 1462, 1507, 1668
Dog catcher, 297
Doing, 20, 206
Done, 27, 28, 59
Door, 280, 411
Dress, 1285
Drinking, 204, 1156, 1349
Drunk, 687, 1080, 1220
Due, 175
Dull, 597
Duty, 916

E

Eager, 529
Ear, 17, 94, 95
Early bird, 66, 1345, 1539
Early riser, 25, 110, 539, 540
Early to bed, 515
Easier said than done, 135, 300, 324, 326, 729

Easy come, easy go, 211, 978, 997, 999, 1011, 1028, 1032
Easy does it, 343
Eating, 18, 202, 203, 204, 309, 1126, 1135, 1423, 1442
Eavesdropping, 551
Economic condition, 563, 974
Education, 337, 353, 575
Effort, 208
Elders, 1546
Emotions, 434
Employees, 1496
End, 943
Ends, 1391
Envious, 1526
Environment, 189
Envy, 295
Erring, 553, 622, 841, 1627
Event, 1197, 1254
Everything goes, 358
Evidence, 394
Evil, 304, 577, 798, 809, 1050, 1260, 1361
Exaggerating, 1204, 1691
Exception, 1177
Excess, 741, 1622
Excretion, 517
Excuses, 52, 268, 481, 1147, 1198
Experience, 307, 330, 449, 525, 533, 644, 660, 770, 854, 880, 1067, 1444
Expert, 902, 1291
Eye for an eye, 5, 35, 228, 1302

F

Face, 213, 842, 1481
Failure, 846, 1360, 1375, 1391
Faint heart, 610, 757, 1293
Fair in love, war, 1247
Faith lost, 752
Fall, 291
Falling, 582
Falling in love, 3, 41
Fame, 25, 251, 1537
Familiarity, 282, 881, 1131, 1309
Family, 707
Fat, 14, 545
Fate, 316, 321, 892

Father, 93, 160, 336, 921
Father-in-law, 1563
Favors, 454, 458, 571, 745, 746, 747, 1077, 1535
Fear, 168, 194, 320, 485
Feathers, 1620
Feelings, 83, 695, 858, 1025, 1249, 1308, 1389
Fiesta, 231
Fight, 567
Figs, 74
Financial straits, 408
Finders, keepers, 980
Fire, 35, 84, 780, 1558
Firearms, 113
First, 92, 573, 575, 628, 1342
Flattery, 1216
Flowers, 1, 973
Folks, 120
Food, 232, 787, 1010
Fools, 339, 792, 911, 932, 1069, 1398, 1626
Foot, 792
Foresight, 509, 612, 1429
Forewarned, 144, 835, 1367
Forgetting, 1272
Forgiving, 614, 896, 1310, 1362, 1627
Fortune, 40, 364, 377, 406, 754, 1206, 1290, 1564
Freedom, 1674
Friday, 360, 481, 716
Friend, 56, 74, 79, 80, 422, 423, 424, 495, 873, 1072, 1107, 1108, 1142, 1235, 1242, 1246, 1266, 1326, 1428, 1437, 1673, 1684, 1690
Friendship, 7, 37, 205, 731, 1404
Frightened, 1424
Frog, 930, 1654
Frugality, 286
Fruit: forbidden, 883, 1239; green ripens, 224
Frustration, 854
Frying pan, 1485, 1486

G

Gain, 96, 334, 981, 1009, 1142, 1230, 1253

Gambler's money, 1032
Getting ahead, 811
Getting even, 115
Getting up early, 1270, 1539
Gifts, 235, 636
Girls, 1173, 1219, 1653
Giving, 57, 58
Giving in, 734
Glory, 733, 775
Gluttons, 309
God, 72, 111, 125, 374, 375, 376, 377, 378, 379, 380, 381, 382, 383, 384, 385, 386, 387, 388, 389, 390, 1445, 1585
Gold, 1110, 1203, 1286, 1287, 1288, 1289, 1312
Golden Rule, 541
Good time, bad time, 1218
Good with bad, 813
Gossips, 439, 1473, 1542
Grass, 117, 188, 436, 589, 772, 884, 1063, 1376, 1523
Great talkers, 771
Greedy, 457, 1477
Greeks, 257, 658
Gruel, 206
Guests, 140, 199, 1687

H

Habit, 502, 526, 577, 759, 760, 761, 1339, 1519
Hair, 1621
Haircut, 1467
Hammering, 226
Hand, 187
Happiness, 133, 1092, 1331, 1569
Hardships, 33
Harming others, 1396
Haste, 101, 284, 344, 1452, 1603, 1688
Having, 99, 273
Head, 158, 1116
Health, 1487, 1686
Heart, 1000, 1191
Heaven, 237, 1341

175

176

177

178

Things: accomplishing, 1590; new, 267; best, 1448; borrowing, 1522; buying, 1226, 1482; cheap, 566, 974, 1017; doing, 164, 173, 289, 985, 1018, 1093, 1094, 1099, 1278, 1279, 1280, 1421, 1544, 1562; evil, 245; first, 18; lending, 990; paying for, 1078; praising, 174, 184; putting off, 331, 1188; signing, 1209; taking care of, 1470; value of, 1225; well done, 1054
Tick (cattle), 4
Time, 675, 676, 677, 678, 679, 680, 681, 715, 1229, 1584
Timid-aggressive, 549, 610, 1293
To err is human, 614
Toil, 1554, 1632
Tongue, 1064, 1065, 1489
Tooth, 64, 228, 1302
Town, 1409
Transitoriness, 431
Travelling, 670
Treatment, 1313, 1340, 1500, 1594
Tree, 112, 317
Trial and error, 421
Trouble, 271, 505, 570, 692, 1013, 1033, 1051
Trust, 19, 80, 481, 537, 558, 605, 657
Truth, 954, 955, 956, 957, 958, 959, 960
Tuesday, 360, 481, 716
Turkey, 9, 119
Turn (good), 81, 828, 1618
Turnip, 287, 1059, 1060
Two cheap as one, 240

U

Unafraid, 546
Uncouth, 498, 1417
Ungrateful, 89, 531, 653, 1222, 1443, 1619, 1695
Unreliable, 1329
Ups and downs, 281, 365, 839

V

Values, 276, 994, 1579

Vanity, 775
Variety, 437
Venom, 1150
Venture, 603, 607, 615, 1456
Vicissitudes, 1504
Viper, 250
Virtue-vice, 962
Visits, 319, 520, 699, 1432
Voice of people, 1689

W

Want, life of, 1119
Water, 27, 28, 29, 30, 63, 255, 276, 314, 385, 783, 1322, 1503
Way, 802, 1134
Wealth, 104
Weather, 748
Welcome, 504
Wet (experience), 660
What will be, 1118
What's done, 351, 1323
Wheel, 611, 1174
Whims, 630, 631
Whistle, 90, 1159, 1172
Widower, 544
Wife, 38, 195, 215, 484, 699, 763, 1148, 1167, 1219
Will, way, 401, 635, 1062, 1186, 1420
Win some, lose some, 1007, 1148
Wind, 271, 384, 996, 1052, 1234
Windfall, 200, 1502
Wine, 392
Wishful thinking, 220
Woman: make up, 217; fair in dark, 335; honest, 907, 1149; lone, 39; married, 906, 1431; married vs. single, 929; mistreated, 39; passionate, 910; quarreling, 275; small, 909; talkative, 945; tall, slender, 905; thin, 861; ugly, 859; well-mannered, 865
Words, 43, 44, 366, 1124, 1320, 1532
Work: antidote for boredom, 1518; attending to, 203; credit for, 1637; children's, 681; doing one's,